Christmas — 1962

298

Christmas — 1962

HORSES

PAUL HAMLYN • LONDON

CONTENTS

PAUL HAMLYN

Westbook House · Fulham Broadway · London

© Copyright Paul Hamlyn Ltd, 1962
Printed in Czechoslovakia
T 924

ABOUT THIS BOOK

No one who is fond of animals can fail to admire the horse, for it combines strength, speed and beauty with intelligence and a friendly, willing temperament.

Because of these qualities, the horse has been, of all animals, man's most constant companion in work and leisure. It has worked his fields, carried him and his belongings from one place to another, borne him on to the battlefield. And for his amusement it has raced, jumped, performed circus tricks, thundered across television and cinema screens, and provided endless hours of enjoyment — with a few, it must be admitted, of discomfort — in the recreation of riding. It has, too, inspired many great artists with its grace and power, and been the subject of some of the finest works of art.

In these pages the horse is presented in all his versatile roles with affection, respect and, we hope, a proper eye for his weaknesses. Our intention is to gain for him a crowd of new admirers, and to entertain, inform and amuse those he already has.

5

THE ORIGIN OF THE
HORSE

Brian Vesey-Fitzgerald

It is commonly accepted that the evolutionary history of the modern horse dates back to the Eocene period in North America: to Eohippus, the Dawn Horse. Indeed, it is often said that the horse has one of the best documented histories of all mammals.

The story goes like this: Eohippus (nowadays more correctly known as Hyracotherium) was a small mammal, about the size of a fox-terrier, which had three toes on the hind feet and four on the front. Eohippus died out, and was succeeded in the Oligocene period by Mesohippus, a somewhat larger animal, which had three toes on each foot. In the Miocene period Mesohippus gave place to Merychippus, again somewhat larger, which also had three toes on each foot, but which apparently used only the central ones for running. In the Pliocene period Merychippus was succeeded by Pliohippus, again a larger animal, which also had three toes on each foot, but only the central ones were visible, the outer pairs being completely covered by skin. Finally, in the Pleistocene period we have the modern horse, *Equus*, with its characteristic hoof.

If this story is true, it is a remarkably clear example, stretching over millions of years, of the way in which an animal adapts itself to its environment and the changing needs of life. There must, of course, have been an even earlier ancestor of the horse than Eohippus, and this animal (of which there is no trace) presumably had five toes like other early mammals. It was the need for increased speed

The zebra is a true wild horse. This is Grévy's zebra, the largest species.

which brought about the loss of toes. As the animal needed to run faster, it got up on to tip-toe for longer and longer periods at a time. This meant that most of its weight was carried on the inner three toes of each foot, the outer ones being lifted off the ground. In the course of millions of years these outer toes became vestigial and finally, with Mesohippus, they disappeared altogether. But the process did not stop there, because the animal, needing still more speed to survive, was still on tip-toe, which meant that most of its weight was now being carried on the central toe of three, the outer ones being lifted free from the ground. In Merychippus (again there has been a lapse of millions of years) the outer toes are useless and, though still visible, are already covered by skin. A few more million years, and in Pliohippus they have disappeared. Even then the process did not end. In the modern horse the outer toes survive only as vestigial splint bones, and the central toe has become a large tough hoof, no longer bearing any resemblance at all to a toe.

If this story is true, it is, indeed, a wonderfully well-documented example of the evolutionary process. But is it true? Maybe the later stages are true enough. But I am far from alone in being sceptical about Eohippus or, if you prefer, Hyracotherium.

The name Eohippus has now been dropped in favour of the name Hyracotherium, which suggests that both names apply to the same animal. But was there just the one animal, the one species? That seems highly improbable to me (and to many others), for Eohippus was an American animal, Hyracotherium a European animal.

In any case Eohippus left no descendants on the American continent. There were no horses in America until the Spaniards brought them in during the sixteenth century. As to Hyracotherium, the name suggests a rodent, and it was, in fact, classed among the rodents until quite recently. All that exists of this animal is one imperfect skull no bigger than that of a rabbit. Upon this skull a vast edifice of theory has been constructed. Seeing only this imperfect skull, Professor Ridgeway confidently asserted that its owner had had four toes on the front feet and three on the hind. He may have been right, of course — who knows? But his confidence was founded upon guesswork, not fact. Seeing only this imperfect skull, W. P. Pycraft confidently asserted that its owner was striped: an exercise in imagination, not a statement of fact. I do not deny that Hyracotherium was the ancestor of the modern horse. I do not know. But I should feel much happier about it if somebody had seen its feet!

In fact, the best that can be said for the theories of the palaeontologists is that they are 'non proven'. In any case they have no bearing on the modern horse and, having been mentioned, are best ignored.

The modern horse, *Equus caballus*, has walked on single hoofs and has shown exactly the same structure as far back as history can trace him; and that is well

An important member of the horse tribe, the donkey

back into the age of prehistoric man. That is a long enough history in all conscience. But it throws no light on origin. It must be said at once (and as categorically as possible) that one cannot make any definite statement as to the origin of the modern horse.

It can be taken as an axiom that once an animal leaves its natural state for the unnatural state of association with man, then the parent stock (the wild stock) becomes extinct. For example, the wild ancestors of the domestic cow and the domestic sheep — there is, of course, a vast difference between a domestic animal and a tame animal — are extinct. There are plenty of wild members of the genus *Equus* in existence today: zebras, asses, even one breed of wild horse. But the animal or animals from which the modern domestic horse sprang are extinct. No one can point with certainty to the parent stock of the modern horse.

Few people, other than specialists, think of the zebra as a horse. But the zebras are, in fact, true wild horses with black or brown stripes on a white or cream ground. (A point of some interest about zebras is that their markings are never exactly the same in any two zebras and are, in fact, never the same on the two sides of any one zebra.) Zebras are confined to Africa, living in herds on plains south of the Sahara. There are three species (though many sub-species): Grévy's Zebra, Burchell's Zebra and the Mountain Zebra.

8

The thoroughbred — the Duke of Norfolk's Optimist — bred for speed

The Arab, noted for its beauty and powers of endurance

The winning ladies' hunter at Dublin Show, 1960

The hackney, a British breed developed from mountain pony stock

Grévy's Zebra, by far the largest, stands about 14 hands, and has the typical neigh of the horse tribe; Burchell's Zebra (there are a number of races) is considerably smaller and more lightly built, has a voice more nearly resembling that of the ass, and is the only one of the zebras that can be tamed, and then only with difficulty; the Mountain Zebra, confined to South Africa and now to one small reserve in the Cradock district, is remarkable for the transverse striping of the hindquarters. Were it not for strict protection, the Mountain Zebra would have followed the Quagga, which lived in the same country of high plateaux and which was striped only on the neck and shoulders, into extinction. The last Quagga died about 1878.

As with zebras, so with asses. There are three wild species (though a number of sub-species or races): the African Wild Ass, the Indian Wild Ass or Onager, and the Tibetan Wild Ass or Kiang. The African Wild Ass is confined to the plains and desert regions of north-east Africa, from Sudan to Somaliland. The Somali race is now to be found only in small numbers in the northern plateau country of Somaliland. They have been strictly protected there for the past forty years or so,

The Mongolian wild horse, known as Przewalski's horse. This mare and foal are in the Munich Zoo

Silver Eagle, a stallion being used to improve the Basuto breed

but show no signs of increase. The Nubian race is also said to be rapidly diminishing in numbers. The Onager lives in herds in north-west India, Baluchistan and Persia. It is hunted for meat and is also said to be diminishing in numbers. The Kiang lives in small herds on the high desert plateau of Tibet, rarely coming below 15,000 feet. The Kiang stands about 12 hands and is much the most horse-like of the asses.

Europe had a wild horse until towards the end of the nineteenth century. This wa the Tarpan, a small dun-coloured animal, which was widely distributed throughout Europe in prehistoric times and which still survived in large herds on the south Russian steppes at the beginning of the nineteenth century. The last one is said to have been shot in 1880. Today there is only one wild horse in exist-ence: the Mongolian Wild Horse, which is perhaps better known as Przewalski's Horse. This is pale dun in colour with a large head — there are a pair at Whip-snade — and is the closest in type of all the wild horses to our domestic breeds. It is confined to the Gobi Desert and little is therefore known about its habits in the wild; but there seems to be little doubt that it, too, is declining in numbers.

It is sometimes said that the Tarpan and the Mongolian Wild Horse are the ancestors of the modern domestic horse. This is certainly not so. It is possible that both may have had some effect on the development of the domestic horses,

14

since the Tarpan would breed with the domestic horses of its neighbourhood as opportunity offered, just as Przewalski's Horse is known to do today. But these are casual, not arranged, matings. There are not many of them and there can never have been very many of them. Their effect, if any, must be very small and certainly cannot have affected the race of domestic horses as a whole.

Let us forget origins, and consider the domestic horse as we know it today. Broadly speaking, it may be divided into two main groups (which must have sprung from two quite distinct foundation stocks): the Northern or Cold-blooded group and the Southern or Hot-blooded group. There is now, of course, a third group which has been formed by the inter-mixture of these two and which is usually known as the Warm-blood group.

The Northern type has a coarse head, generally large, with a Roman nose, a short thick neck, large teeth and a tail set low on rather drooping hindquarters. The temperament is phlegmatic. This is the horse of the prehistoric cave-paintings and is invariably depicted with a short erect mane like that of the ass. This Northern group is represented today in our heavy horse breeds (the Shire and so forth) and in some of the European pony breeds, notably (in the British Isles) by the Exmoor Pony and the Shetland Pony.

The Southern type has a small head, usually with a dished face, a long arched neck, small teeth, and a tail set high on hindquarters which do not droop. The

The Australian Waler, 'an athletic aristocrat'.
Reproduced by kind permission of the Australian News and Information Bureau

15

temperament is the reverse of phlegmatic, being highly strung and fiery. Even in the earliest paintings the mane is never depicted as short and erect, but as long and flowing. Today the typical example of this Southern type is the pure-bred Arab.

It is rather more difficult to point to a typical example of the intermediary warm-blood group, for there has been so much crossing between the two main groups. For example, the Southern blood has been introduced from time to time even into some of our heavy breeds, and almost all our mountain pony breeds now carry a large admixture of Southern blood. And this has happened all over the world. Moreover, there can be no doubt that climate has played a great part in the development of the various breeds of domestic horse. When, for example, Southern blood has been introduced into members of the Northern group living in cold climates — as has been done from time to time in the case of the Norwegian Pony, the Iceland Pony, the Lithuanian Zemaitukas, and so forth — it has had comparatively little effect on type and practically none on temperament. When it has been introduced into members of the Northern group living in more equable climates the effect has sometimes been quite dramatic. The Welsh Mountain Pony, for example, has been transformed from a quite ordinary coarse Northern type mountain pony into one of the most beautiful creatures in the world.

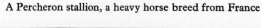

A Percheron stallion, a heavy horse breed from France

Jutlander dray horses from Denmark

Bearing these qualifications in mind, perhaps it might be said that the Thorough-bred is today the most typical example of the Warm-blood group. There are those who maintain that the Thoroughbred is pure-bred Arab. But this is simply not true. What is true is that the Thoroughbred is almost entirely of foreign, but not necessarily of Southern, blood. All Thoroughbreds trace their ancestry, on the male side, to three Arab sires: the Darley Arabian, the Godolphin Arabian and the Byerley Turk. But what mares were used? Certainly they were not pure-bred Arab mares. Probably they were English mares (that is, mares of basically Northern type) with some Southern blood in them. It is often forgotten that we were importing Italian horses, which undoubtedly had a good deal of Arab in them, as early as the beginning of the sixteenth century. Be that as it may, there can be no doubt that very little Arab blood has been used since the early days. This is because the value of the Thoroughbred lies in its speed. The Arab has remarkable powers of endurance, but it is not particularly fast and cannot compare with the Thoroughbred in any test of speed. So great is the emphasis on speed that a Thoroughbred not fast enough to win on the racecourse has little value and is discarded, most of the colts being gelded. The mares, however, are much used for crossing with other breeds to produce hunters and hacks.

17

The Norwegian pony

English Thoroughbred blood has gone all over the world. Racehorses through-out the world are basically of English Thoroughbred blood, but Thoroughbred stallions have also been much used abroad to improve the quality of native breeds. And this is true also of the Arab. Indeed, so much has this been done that it is now a little difficult to point to pure breeds among horses (though there are still a number of pure pony breeds, especially among northern mountain ponies); most of them, despite a breed name, are in fact part-bred, for most of them now contain an admixture of Arab or Thoroughbred blood. And, it must be remem-bered, the Thoroughbred itself is, originally, a 'manufactured' breed. Moreover, there are some 'breeds' which, though they bear a breed name, are not really breeds at all, but colour varieties. For example, the Palomino, recognised in North

Icelandic ponies. *Reproduced by kind permission of the Iceland Tourist Bureau*

The Dartmoor pony

America as a breed, is actually a colour variety; palomino colouring turns up regularly in horse breeds all over the world. Another example of this is the Pinto, the 'Painted Horse' of North America, which is also recognised there as a breed and has its breed society. In Britain, we know these horses as piebald or skewbald, a colour variety, which may occur in any breed.

Nevertheless, every great horse-breeding country in the world has what may be described as its native breeds, which, though they may contain Arab or Thoroughbred blood, are yet, because of the effect of climatic conditions, quite distinct in type. For example, there are no native horses in the Americas, in Australia or in South Africa. The horses in these countries have all been introduced by man — to the Americas in the sixteenth century, to Australia and South Africa at a much later date — and, in origin, are as mongrel as could be, having been developed from the fusion of many breeds. But, in each case, climate and natural surroundings have exercised influence and distinct breeds have developed.

For example, the Criollo of South America has developed from horses brought in by the Spaniards at the time of the conquest. These horses included Arabs and

Barbs used by the officers, the small Spanish horses used by the rank-and-file of the cavalry, and pack horses. Many of these escaped and roamed in herds on the pampas and elsewhere, inter-breeding freely. Climate and natural selection (only the toughest animals surviving) played their part, and the result is the Criollo, a breed recognisable at sight anywhere. The Mustang of western North America sprang from precisely the same stock, but is quite different in appearance because it has developed under different climatic conditions.

I suppose that the characteristic breed of South Africa is the Basuto Pony. This animal, though no one would think so to look at it, originated in a cross of Arab and Barb blood brought in by the Dutch. Later, towards the end of the eighteenth century and early in the nineteenth, good English Thoroughbred blood was used. The result of all this ought to be a magnificent Thoroughbred type. The Basuto is a small thick-set pony of great strength and almost infinite endurance. Climate and natural conditions have modified type.

The Australian Waler has been developed from exactly the same strains as the Basuto pony: Arab and Barb blood, and later the best of Thoroughbred blood.

The Highland pony

Time off from work

Left: A mare and foal at the National Stud

It would be difficult to imagine two animals of the same stock less alike. The Waler looks an athletic aristocrat: the Basuto a tough workman. Again climate and natural surroundings — in this case the grazing especially — have proved the dominating factor.

But the Middle East, Asia north of the Himalayas, and Europe are the great and natural horse-breeding lands of the world; and it is in these lands that one finds the greatest diversity of breeds. I have not the space to list them all; suffice it to say that each country has one or more breeds, which are distinctive to that country or region and which have a history going back, in many cases, for centuries. In the Middle East, the Arab, the Barb and the Persian; in Asia, the Mongolian particularly (though there are many others); in Europe — well, in Europe every country has one or more national breeds. In Italy, the Neaopolitan; in France, the Boulonnais, the Breton, the Percheron (all heavy horses); in Belgium, the Ardennes and the Brabancon (both heavy horses); in Austria, the Lippizana; in Hungary, the Shagya; in Germany, the Hanoverian, the Mecklenburg and the Oldenburg; in Poland, the Konik; in Russia, the Orloff and many others.

The Shetland pony

Connemara ponies

But, for its size, the British Isles have more breeds of horses and ponies than any other country in the world. Consider only our mountain ponies: the Connemara, the Dartmoor, the Exmoor, the Fell, the Highland, the Western Isles, the New Forest, the Shetland, the Welsh. It is an astonishing list for so small a country. Of course, many of these mountain pony breeds would have passed into extinction long ago but for the efforts of enthusiasts and it is idle to pretend that some of them today have much resemblance to the original breed whose name they bear. The Dartmoor and the New Forest, for example, have been much 'improved' by outside blood, since these are in great demand as riding ponies. And the Welsh, of course, has been changed enormously by the skilful use of Arab blood. We have, too, developed from our mountain pony stock three quite distinctive, and typically British, pony breeds: the Dales (which resembles a heavy horse in miniature), the Hackney and the Welsh Cob. What may be described as our 'native' light horse is the Cleveland Bay, which has been much used with the Thoroughbred to produce hunters of high quality. From the Cleveland Bay there was also developed a draught-horse of great quality, the Yorkshire Coach, which, as the name implies, was once used for drawing the mail and passenger coaches. Another typical product of the English breeder is the Anglo-Arab, a pure cross of Arab and Thoroughbred; an animal of great beauty and one of the best riding-horses in the world. We have, too, our heavy horses: the Shire, the Clydesdale, the Suffolk Punch, and the Percheron, a comparatively recent import from France, which English breeders and English conditions have altered a good deal.

Of all these many breeds only the Yorkshire Coach and the heavy horses are in any danger, even in this age of mechanisation. The Yorkshire Coach exists today only because of the devotion of a few enthusiasts, for there is now no use

24

for a draught-horse of its type. The heavy horse breeds, whose primary use is on farm-land, must inevitably decrease in numbers in face of the competition of the tractor; but there is no prospect of their complete extinction. All the rest, so it seems to me, face a bright future; much brighter than one would have dreamed possible even ten years ago. For the more mechanised our lives become, the more urgent is our need to seek relaxation with animals.

A British cross-bred horse, the Anglo-Arab

An Improvisation on Illustrations from

ADVENTURES IN SEARCH OF A
HORSE

(published in 1836)

1 A gentleman of breeding deserves a horse of breeding

2 A willing animal of co-operative temperament, a credit to his stable

3 A consistent, predictable horse, not prone to inner thoughts and doubts

4 A placid beast, undisturbed and unruffled by sudden alarms and excursions

5 With the stamina and determination to travel long distances in all conditions

6 With no tendency to self-display which might cause public embarrassment

7 And one that will demonstrate affection for its master at all times and in all places . . .

HORSES IN
SPORT

Denzil Batchelor   Presumably the first thing man did with a horse was to eat it; the second thing to break it; but the third thing was to make it into a collaborator in the field of sport. Teaching it to jump and to participate in a ball game came later — the first step was to get the animal to take part in races.

You could ride it, or you could drive it. The four-horse chariot race was on the programme as early as the 23rd Olympiad (688 B.C.) and the race with mounted horses was admitted to the thirty-third — forty years later. Still later came mule races and loose-horse races. From the description of Pausanias the Spartan it is believed that the original course was 1,600 feet by 400, divided by an earth bank with a turning-post at each end: and from Pindar we learn that as many as forty chariots might compete in one race.

'Here comes Charlie! Let's have a rubber of bridge.'
Reproduced by kind permission of Methuen & Co. Ltd

...the third thing man did with the horse was to train it for sport

In Ancient Rome the chariot race was from the fourth century B.C. the chief attraction of the circus, the only public spectacle at which men and women were allowed to mingle in the audience. Chariots started in an oblique line, and made seven circuits of the course, there being up to twenty-four races a day. Drivers were generally slaves, wearing different colours, while their horses were imported from Sicily, Spain and Cappadocia. In the first races between mounted horses, each rider was given two mounts, leaping from one to the other during the race.

It was the Romans who introduced the horse-race into Gaul — and into Britain; though some of the Germanic tribes indulged in the sport from time immemorial as part of their religious practices. The Christian Church frowned on the early horse-races — the first Council of Arles declared that those who took part should be denied Communion. But racing took root throughout Europe, and in the twelfth century William Fitzstephen writes of a meeting held every Friday in Smithfield, while in the reign of Coeur de Lion knights raced at Whitsuntide over a three-mile course for 'forty pounds of ready gold'.

But it was the Stuarts who brought organised racing into the British way of life. On Wednesday, 27 February 1605, James I killed six hares hunting near Newmarket, enjoyed a picnic lunch behind a bush, fell in love with the neighbourhood and returned to it frequently to stay at the Griffin Inn, whence he gave his Court a chance to enjoy the sport of horse-racing he had learned to like in Scotland. Then Charles II made Newmarket his favourite resort, introduced regular Spring and Autumn meetings, founded the Royal Plates, rode in matches himself, and had the Rowley Mile named after him — for didn't all England know him by his nickname of Old Rowley?

Such were the modest origins. Newmarket became, and has remained, the headquarters of the turf in Britain: and the British turf became and has remained the crowning glory of equine sport throughout the world, as Wimbledon is of lawn tennis and Lord's of cricket — however completely players from the far ends of the earth may eclipse the British at these particular sports. But there are other peaks on the skyline. The greates race in the world is the mile-and-a-half Epsom

The greatest race in the world — the Derby (1961 winner Psidium)

Ascot, the Fern Hill Stakes, won in 1961 by Violetta III

Derby for three-year-olds, first run in 1780; the most elegant meeting is Royal Ascot, with the two-and-a-half mile Ascot Gold Cup, first run in 1807, as the highlight of the meeting.

Certainly it was not till the second half of the nineteenth century that it was ever really considered possible that the best of English thoroughbreds could be seriously challenged for supremacy. But in 1865 a French horse Gladiateur, owned by a son of one of Napoleon's generals, won the Triple Crown — Guineas, Derby and St Leger — despite a vast enlargement of one of the joints of his off fore-leg as the result of having been trodden on while a foal.

In 1876 Kisber, a Hungarian-bred colt, won the Derby, and £100,000 in bets for his owner. Iroquois — though the son of a sire imported from England — won for America in 1881. Orby (1907) and Trigo (1929) were Irish-bred winners of the greatest Classic. More recently British predominance has been far more seriously challenged. Since the war there have been five Derby winners from France.

But, by and large, the history of the Derby is the history of the British thoroughbred at its greatest. The supreme champions have, of course, won not only the supreme three-year-old Classic, but also the other two as well: the mile-long Two Thousand Guineas for colts (the fillies have their Thousand Guineas), and the mile-and-three-quarter St Leger.

But the Derby comes first. Its history is full of romances and high fantasy. In 1844 Running Rein was first past the post, being ultimately disqualified when it was discovered that he was a four-year-old, disguised to escape recognition with the help of ladies' hair-dye bought from Mr Rossi's shop near Regent Street. Then there was 1867 when Mr Henry (afterwards Lord) Chaplin's Hermit won after snow had fallen right up until the starter dropped his flag, despite breaking a blood-vessel a week before the race. The Marquis of Hastings, who a few years previously had eloped with the woman Henry Chaplin had been engaged to marry, lost £100,000 wagered against the success of the man he had wronged: it was said that Hermit had 'half-destroyed a Marquisate'.

31

Then there was 1913: the year a suffragette flung herself under the King's horse at Tattenham Corner; and Cragonour, first past the post, was disqualified on an objection of the Stewards, and the race was given to the 100-1 outsider, Aboyeur.

The history of the greatest race in the world has many such fabulous stories. And of course it is blazoned with great names: the unbeaten Ormonde, the mighty Flying Fox, Rock Sand and Bahram among winners of the Triple Crown. (It is sad that the great St Simon could not be a starter in the race.) There are jockeys like Steve Donoghue who won the race six times, including two war-time substitutes; and Sir Gordon Richards (twenty-six times champion jockey) who won only once, on Pinza, and who is one of the mightiest champions of recent years. Fred Archer, reputed to have come round Tattenham Corner with his left leg over the rails, won the race five times; Buckle and Custance, Sam Chifney and Fordham are all there — and in recent years Johnstone, Elliott, Smirke, Lester Piggott and Harry Carr are among the immortals. Great winning trainers include Matt Dawson, John Porter, Fred Darling (who had six winners), Noel Murless, Cecil Boyd-Rochfort, and Harry Wragg.

Of course, the Derby is only one race in the English programme: there are plenty of others, down to the smallest Selling Plates on the most obscure courses — we spend nearly £400 million a year betting on horses.

Racing in New York, at the Aqueduct race track, 1950

Flat racing in New Zealand — one of their favourite sports

But while British bloodstock is the pride and glory of the equine world, and while there is an insular belief that racing is first and foremost *our* national sport, it is idle to imagine that our example in this field has been merely followed in a childishly imitative way by 'certain lesser breeds without the law'. No one can seriously believe this who has noted the innumerable French triumphs in the twentieth century at Newmarket, Epsom and Ascot, or who has seen such superb Italian champions as Nearco, Botticelli, Tissot, or Ribot, which won the King George VI and Queen Elizabeth Stakes in 1956 (a year in which we did not get a horse into the first three in the Derby or the Oaks).

Perhaps our eyes were re-opened to American class by the overwhelming defeat of our Derby-winner Papyrus by Zev in 1923; and in recent years the least sporting reader of the daily papers cannot fail to be apprised of the tremendous achievements on our turf of Australian jockeys — Carslake and Bullock, Johnstone, Frank Wootton, 'Scobie' Breasley, Edgar Britt and many others. It's a pity that we've not had as much opportunity to meet their champion horses — Carbine, Phar Lap, Peter Pan — as we have had of getting to know their riders.

Perhaps the result of the $70,000 1960 Laurel International epitomised the global situation in modern racing. There were starters from the States, England, Ireland, France, Italy and Russia. Bald Eagle, an American entry, won the race for the second time. Russian horses were third and fourth. In the field of eleven,

33

The toughest race of them all — the Grand National. Shown here in the lead is Merryman II, winner in 1960, who was bought for £200 as a hunter

the English horses were ninth and tenth — they were only not last and last-but-one because a French horse threw his jockey at the start and took no part in the race.

A glance at this event warrants the focusing of attention on the American attitude to horse-racing. The first thing to be noted is that the spectator in the States is given the most luxurious treatment; and that Americans consider a visit to the races in Britain an alternative to slumming. For far less than he may pay to stand out of sight of the race in England, the spectator is given a comfortable seat from which he can see every yard of each of the sixty-three standardised oval courses. He can back his horse to win, to finish first or second, or to be in the first three.

Moreover, he sees wonderful racing for his (very little) money. The smallest race is worth £1,000. There is a £10,000 race every day. The Kentucky Derby (to describe which, according to Irving S. Cobb, 'you'd need a larynx of spun silver and the tongue of an anointed angel') was worth £40,000 as long ago as Citation's year. Citation . . . there was a horse to pin-point the difference between English and American training methods! When an English horse breaks down he is usually automatically retired. Not so Citation. He was patched up, rested, and put back into training.

Then again, look at the frequency with which the hardy American stock is raced. Many English experts think there is a lot to be said for not racing two-year-olds at all — certainly no more often than two or three times in the season. Well, the

34

great Seabiscuit, one of the most famous horses in American history, ran some forty times as a two-year-old.

Of course, American racehorses are bigger, tougher, more powerful, but less endowed with high quality than are ours. Theory sometimes suggests that — since speed is the one quality insisted on — American thoroughbreds must lack stamina. But Flares (winner in 1938) and Omaha (just beaten in '36) were two of the mighty stars in Ascot Gold Cup history. There was nothing wrong with the stamina of Man o' War, or of War Admiral his son (winner of the Preakness, Kentucky Derby and Belmont Stakes), or of Battleship, another son which won the Grand National.

And there is nothing wrong with the stamina of leading American jockeys either. Eddie Arcaro, only son of a man who ran successively a music-store, a taxicab and a removal business, became a jockey after being fired as an incompetent caddy. His riding of Lawrin in the Kentucky Derby of 1938 was described as a masterpiece by Damon Runyan, and Ivor Anthony said of him: 'That is a great jockey, any time and in any country.' Arcaro won over £3 million in stakes in eight years. His chief rivals among the supreme American jockeys have been English-born Johnny Longden and Tod Sloan, who introduced the 'monkey crouch' to revolutionise English racing in 1897.

Yes, the Americans have made history on the turf — and the Irish and the French too. Only last season the French took over £78,000 and the Irish over

Oxo, winner of the Grand National in 1959, looks tired out as he takes the last fence

In the Grand National, even the first fence takes its toll

£65,000 from British racecourses. Ballymoss, trained by Vincent O'Brien, winner of the St Leger in '57 and the £23,642 King George and Queen Elizabeth Stakes in '58, was the greatest horse from Ireland we have ever seen — only bad luck prevented him from winning the Laurel International in America.

As for the French, well, from the moment World War II ended their champions were into their stride. Owners like M. Boussac and Mme. Volterra captured the global imagination as the late Aga Khan and Aly Khan captured it in their time. Mme. Suzy Volterra was a particularly fascinating figure. Her husband, Léon Volterra, nursed a lifelong ambition to win the English Derby. In 1954 he had the chance of a lifetime with Amour Drake; but his health was so bad that his doctor would not allow him to go to Epsom to see the race. He heard it on the wireless in his flat in Paris, and the story the press published was that when his horse was crowded out by Swallow Tail and the jockey switched inside in the last furlong to fail by inches in the final stride, the shock was too great for him and he died of a heart attack. But on the day she came out of mourning, sitting on the sofa on which he had died, Mme. Volterra told me the true story. Her husband's heart attack had occurred just before the start: he did not recover consciousness till a few seconds after the finish. She held out her arms and said: 'Léon, you've won the Derby.' And *then* he died.

It is nice to know that her (and his) ambition was only delayed. Six years later she won the Derby with Phil Drake.

The greatest of all French horses in France's Golden Age, since the end of the war, was probably the late Aly Khan's Petite Etoile, winner of the Thousand Guineas and the Oaks in 1959; perhaps not a real middle distance champion but unsurpassably brilliant over any slightly shorter course. French trainers like Head, Carter and Semblat and jockeys like Doyasbere and Poincelet most certainly have

36

made their mark on the English turf. In the first dozen years since World War II France won six Ascot Gold Cups — they had not previously won this event since Massine's victory in 1924. Caracalla II, an odds-on winner in '46, was perhaps their best stayer in this testing event.

The French challenge on the flat — the Irish challenge over jumps . . . That is the way of the world: the racing world.

Anything to make a tough sport harder — that is the way what Swinburne calls 'the holy spirit of man' goes into action. Flat racing was a severe enough test for any man born of woman — so of course (especially as in England you can only go flat-racing between April and early November) somebody had to invent steeple-chasing. And, of course, that somebody had to be an Irishman; though even the old MS in the possession of the O'Briens of Dromoland is silent as to whether it was Mr O'Callaghan or Mr Edmund Blake who issued the challenge that led to the very first steeplechase in 1752 over four and a half miles of country between the Church of St Buttevant and the spire of St Leger Church. In 1803 'the first regular steeplechase' took place in Ireland, inspired by a hunt dinner. Records are silent on the subject of the place, course, or runners — but it is known that the 'added money' was a hogshead of claret, a pipe of port and a quarter-cask of rum.

'The Druid' mentions a far from 'regular' steeplechase run in Leicestershire in 1792, over the eight miles from Barkby Holt to the Coplow and back. History records that the horse that finished second was 'rather fat', while the rider of the favourite was invited to save a hundred yards by going through a friend's garden and jumping a gate into the road. In those days, of course, a steeplechase was a race from one church steeple to another, taking the best line you could find.

But though there were English matches of twenty miles and more around the time of Waterloo, the Irish still blazed the trail. There was the great race of the

Two well-taken jumps at the Vine Hunt point-to-point

period at Lismore, for example, when the betting was evens that there would be six falls among the field of six — no one bothered to quote odds against any individual starter winning. In fact, the winner fell four times and the contemporary report cheerfully adds: 'in all, twelve falls, but nobody killed.'

The sport grew in popularity through the eighteen-thirties: the Cheltenham meetings began around 1833, and three years later Liverpool held its first, the opening event being won by Captain Becher, 'the last of the leather breeches', who had been forbidden as a boy to ride a donkey lest he should become expert on such a mount and never bother to become a horseman. Becher never won a National, but in the first of all, in 1839, he fell into the brook that still bears his name, thus gaining an immortality denied Jem Mason and Lottery, the great race's original winner, which won races at sixteen and was subsequently put to pull a plough.

Oh, the horses that have won at Aintree! There was Moifaa, the seventeen-hand New Zealander that looked like a starved elephant and won the National of 1904 after reaching England by swimming ashore from a shipwreck. There was Roquefort (1885) which had once drawn a dogcart and Glenside (1911) which had only one eye. There was Rubio in 1908 — the first American-bred winner, foaled in

Ladies' Races are a major event at every point-to-point meeting

Hugh Wiley on Nautical at the White City in 1959

A race meeting at Brighton Race Course, Sussex

Winning pair of ponies at the Royal Windsor Horse Show, 1960

Left: Mrs Brenda Williams on Little Model, who represented Great
Britain in the Dressage event at the Olympic Games

California and sold as a two-year-old at Newmarket for fifteen guineas, which broke
down so badly that he was put into a hotel bus to meet the trains at Towcester,
an exercise which was thought to have improved his condition to such an extent that
he was considered fit to be put back into training. There was Battleship which had
stood at stud before winning at Aintree and was the second American-bred horse
to win, carrying Bruce Hobbs, a seventeen-year-old jockey.

There are the mighty champions which have won two Grand Nationals. Let
their names by blazoned. First comes Abd-El-Kader (a 15 hand 2 inch pony with
a dam that had pulled the Salisbury coach), which won in 1850 and 1851. The
Lamb triumphed in 1868 and 1871, his owner having dreamed of his later victory —
seeing his own cerise and blue in the dream quite vividly, to the confusion of all
subsequent investigators who deny that you can dream in Technicolour.

The Colonel, winner in '69 and '70, had Exmoor ponies in his sire's pedigree and
a half-bred dam. Manifesto is thought by many to be the greatest horse that ever
won over Aintree's 4 miles 856 yards, and 30 fences. He won in '97 and '99, up
to the last fence seemed likely to win in 1900, and was also placed in 1902. There

The American horse Greyhound — one of the fastest trotters of all time

Trotting is not a popular sport as yet in Britain, but here is a trotting meet held in Kent

was Poethlyn (once sold for £15), the winner in 1918 and 1919; and Reynoldstown which carried 12 st 2 lb in his second successive victory — both his wins he was ridden by Gentlemen Riders, Messrs Furlong and Walwyn of the 9th Lancers.

Which has been the greatest of post-war winners? Perhaps the choice would lie between the three successive victors (1953-5) trained by the incredible O'Brien in Ireland: Early Mist, Royal Tan and Quare Times. Or perhaps it might be the game Mr What (1958), one of two eight-year-olds to win in twenty years. But probably the most remarkable was Merryman II, the 1960 winner, owned by Miss Winifred Wallace of Edinburgh who bought him for £200 as a hunter and won three point-to-points on him. He was the third winner trained by Neville Crump, the first clear favourite to win in thirty-three years, and the only horse ever to win the treble: the Foxhunters' Chase, the Grand National and the Scottish Grand National.

I have mentioned two outstanding American winners in Rubio and Battleship, a New Zealander in Moifaa: but we must not forget Lutteur III, a five-year-old stallion, which won for France in 1909. These victories (and even the Irish ascendancy in the race) are the more remarkable because nowhere in the world are there steeplechase courses to compare in severity with either Aintree or Cheltenham. But the most forlorn hope, not of winning but of completing the course, is enough to lure runners from all quarters of the globe: a year or two ago there were even entries from the U.S.S.R. neither of which had any chance of getting over more than a few jumps.

44

Steeplechasing at its best remains a closed shop for English and Irish horses, trainers and jockeys. Among the latter must be mentioned Bryan Marshall, winner on Early Mist and Royal Tan, T. Taaffe and F. Winter.

Hurdling is a less popular and less well-rewarded branch of racing than steeple-chasing — the two-mile Champion Hurdle Cup was first competed for at Chelten-ham as recently as 1927. Once again, O'Brien is one of the supreme trainers in the sport's history: his Hatton's Grace won the event thrice (1949-51) to be directly followed by Sir Ken, trained by W. Stephenson during his hat-trick of victories — the great T. Malony rode Hatton's Grace in his last victory and Sir Ken in all his wins.

Long ago the Badminton Library wrote that 'it would be difficult to justify hurdle-racing as a means of sport leading to a desirable end!' quoting the view of a member of the Jockey Club and of the National Hunt Committee that 'the chief merit of hurdle-racing is that it does not pretend to have any *raison d'être* except the encouragement of gambling, and it answers this purpose admirably'.

A trotting race at Goshen, N. Y., for two-year-olds

Setting off for the hunt on a misty morning

No one could level a similar accusation at point-to-point racing. It is the major glory of the countryman's (and countrywoman's) life; and it owes its existence to the hunting field. It is essentially a family affair: and the Ladies Races are major occasions in every meeting — though in Ireland the ladies are allowed to compete on level terms with men in open races. Many great steeplechasers have first learned the facts of life at point-to-points, and some have gone back to them in the evening of their careers. Such sport is to racing what the village game is to cricket: the most charming, merry and exciting form of the sport — unmarred by financial considerations that turn more important occasions from red letter days into days of reckoning. And if John Masefield glorified steeplechasing in his poem *Right Royal*, Siegfried Sassoon has immortalised the no less tense and thrilling point-to-point in his prose.

Trotting makes little impact on the British racing-man, and pony racing has no very large following. But the former sport is immensely popular in the United States and Australia (where respectively Titan Hanover and Walla Walla are revered names), and pony racing has had a long history Down Under where it is colloquially known as 'the Mackers' — macaronis being rhyming slang for ponies. Russian trotting horses have in recent years shown impressive form in Norway.

But apart from flat-racing and jumping races, rural Britain's chief interest in the horse as a sporting proposition is concentrated on hunting.

Hunting is as old as Homer, but when the sons of Autolycus went forth on the chase up the steep hill of wood-clad Parnassus, the goodly Odysseus 'swaying his

46

long spear' surely followed hounds on foot. But when in the third century A.D., Appian described the chase in Ancient Green he demands: 'Give me young men who are not over-stout. For the hunter must mount the noble horse amid the rocks, anon must leap a ditch.' So it was in the beginning — and so it has continued, with some emphasis from its defenders on its uplifting and ennobling qualities. Gaston de Foix in 1387 declared that 'hunting causeth a man to eschew the seven deadly sins . . . men are better when riding, more just and understanding...'

In England when Kings hunted in the past, they chased the stag — a sport still flourishing on Exmoor — and it was not till half-way through the eighteenth century that fox-hunting became part and parcel of English country life. It is generally predicted during war that hunting is too expensive a sport to survive, but in these days of inflation and crippling taxation there are more packs than ever — nearly 200 in England and Wales alone, though the cost of running a pack which hunts three days a week varies from a few hundred a year in the Fells to £6,000 or more in the Shires (Leicestershire, Rutland and Northamptonshire).

Hunting on horseback isn't, of course, exclusively British. It is to be found in parts of the United States, Australia, New Zealand and France; but in this field Britain unquestionably leads the world. Its 'marvellous system of hunt organization,' says J. B. Thomas, an American M.F.H., 'is the direct result of British continuity of policy intelligently handed down in many instances from father to son through numerous generations.'

The sport is ferociously attacked on the grounds of its cruelty by many of the present generation. Those who champion it claim (with the support of the R. S. P. C. A.) that there is no less cruel way of keeping foxes in check; those who attack it consider the hounding to death of a small animal by packs of hounds followed by hordes of festively attired men and women to be unsporting and barbaric. William Somervile summed up one point of view in *The Chase* (1735):

'. . . the Sport of Kings;
Image of War, without its guilt.'

Oscar Wilde spoke for the other side when he wrote of 'the unspeakable in pursuit of the uneatable'. A townsman would not presume to pass judgment.

In the dear, dead days before World War I a cavalry officer hunted in the winter, played polo in the summer and studied Clausewitz in between. Polo cannot be as old as flat-racing, for the ball game is not as old as the race, but its origins are lost in the mists of antiquity. Perhaps the Persians were the first to play it, many centuries before Christ; perhaps the Tibetans, or the Chinese. British planters from Assam brought it back to India (where it had already once withered) half-way through the nineteenth century; and Army officers soon made a fetish of it. A report in *The Field* inspired the 10th Hussars to have a shot at the game in England, with hockey sticks and a cricket bat. In 1871 the first full-scale match — six aside until 1882, thereafter four aside — was played in England between the 10th Hussars and the 9th Lancers, and a quarter-century later the game became popular in America, where the offside rule was abolished in 1907, as a few years later was the height limit for ponies of 14 hands 2 inches. Today the world's great polo-playing countries are the United States and the Argentine — no other countries could live with them over eight seven-and-a-half minute chukkas on the 300 yard by 160 yard boarded field. England won the Westchester Cup against U.S.A. in 1900, 1902 and 1914 — since then America have won six times without losing a game. One reason is that the side that can afford the best ponies has a great advantage — but that is only one reason.

In 1937 a remarkable team of brothers, the Ashtons from Goulburn, Australia, came to England and won the Champion Cup.

The post-war revival in the game in this country has been largely due to the efforts of Lord Cowdray. Its success has been not unconnected with the public's wish to see (and if possible) hear the Duke of Edinburgh playing. He has developed into one of the better British players now in the game.

The most popular polo player, the Duke of Edinburgh, in action at Cowdray Park

An exciting moment in a polo tournament at Roehampton — an almost certain goal is saved at the ast moment

The most popular equine sport — racing apart — with the English townsman was almost unknown a quarter-century ago, though records show that competitive show-jumping was in existence at least as far back as the beginning of the century. But show-jumping is the sport which has increased in popularity more than any other since the end of World War II, largely because of its introduction to the general public through television. The victory of the British team in the 1952 Olympic Games at Helsinki added to the sport's poularity, and Colonel Harry Llewellyn and Foxhunter, Wilf Whyte and the pig-rooting Nizefella, and Miss Pat Smythe on Prince Hal or Tosca in course of time became figures in Britain's national folklore.

It is sometimes said that television has at last sated the public taste for show-jumping, but the fact is that the attendances in this year's Royal International Horse Show broke all records. There are said to be some ten thousand riders in all classes of show-jumping in Britain, and though no one can be quite sure of the reason, the sport remains more popular with girls than with boys.

Well, we have come a long way since the Chariot races of the 23rd Olympiad, since the pre-historic days when man first made the horse his partner in the sporting field. As far as I know, no one has ever staged swimming-races or skating races with horses as competitors. There have been boxing kangaroos but no boxing horses, and horses have yet to race unmounted for gold cups, or to chase mechanical carrots — but in pretty well every other field they have collaborated with their masters to add beauty and thrills to the sporting scene.

'Give a man a horse he can ride,' as the poem said . . .

INTERNATIONAL SHOW JUMPING STARS

1 Wilf White on Nizefela (G.B.)

2 Col. Llewellyn on Foxhunter (G.B.)

3 Hans Winkler on Halla (Germany)

4 Capt. Raimondo D'Inzeo on Merano (Italy)   5 Capt. Barry on Hollyford (Ireland)

6 Comdt. Manuel Ordovas on Bohemio (Spain)

7 H. Wiley on Nautical (U.S.A.)   8 P. Jonqueres D'Oriola on Arlequin (France)

Not every attempt ends in success

...but the less said about these the better!

THE
SPANISH RIDING SCHOOL
OF VIENNA

Peter Roberts   Every day the bustling Reitschul Strasse in Vienna has a traffic block. From seven o'clock in the morning, and thereafter at forty-five minute intervals, a policeman holds up the long stream of cars for a few moments to allow a string of magnificent horses to pass under the archway which connects the Spanish Riding School with its stables on the other side of the road . . .

As one enters the great ring at ground level, the impact of the long, high colonnade with its dramatic perspective conveys the dignity and grandeur of the school, which adjoins the old Imperial Palace. At the far end, the Imperial box stands, still with its portrait of the founder, a portrait that is saluted by every rider whenever he enters the ring itself. Above the Renaissance Corinthian columns runs a balcony backed by a clear-story of rich design.

At ground level, under the Royal Box, is the distinguished visitors' enclosure, from where they can watch displays by the school. A custom of the riders on such occasions is to ride in single file into the visitors' box and canter around them in a

An exhibition by the Spanish Riding School of Vienna at the International Horse Show, White City, 1953

'Perfect harmony between man and horse'.

tight circle before the display — a tradition which has often disconcerted many prominent visitors!

Such, then, is the setting for this the most famous of all riding schools, an establishment whose very name is the quintessence of all that is skilful and good in the high art of horsemanship.

'*As far as the art of riding is concerned, all nations have their particular rules and principles which vary more or less; what one nation considers good another considers bad . . .*' So wrote Adam von Weytother, Riding Master at the Austrian Court in 1789. We now consider that good riding follows the principles given to us by the Spanish Riding School of Vienna, founded over half a century earlier by the Emperor Charles the Sixth.

Although this school has become known as the Spanish Riding School (due not to the nationality of the riders but to the breed of horses used in it), its home has always been in Vienna, a home that has survived the countless hazards of European strife, has outlived the Austro-Hungarian Empire, and has continued through two World Wars.

Formed as a replica of the great Riding Academy of Versailles in France (which was disbanded during the French Revolution), it has now eclipsed all other establishments in renown. Its methods have remained constant through at least two hundred years; its standard-work by François de la Guérinière of the École de Cavalerie has been its mainstay throughout the centuries.

The Horses

Lipizza is a small village — it once belonged to Austria — on the Adriatic coast, and it is here that, until World War I, the horses used exclusively by the Spanish Riding School were bred. Of Spanish origin, the horses are still known as Lippizaners, although the stud is now in Piber, which nestles in the Styrian Range in Southern Austria.

The stallions are represented by five ancient families; Pluto, Maestoso, Conversano, Neapolitano and Favory, and their offspring are known by one of these names

55

The *Spanish Trot*

coupled with the name of the dam. The foals are taken up into the nearby hills to range free until their fourth year, when they are directed to the stables of the Spanish School in Vienna to begin their long training.

Why do they use only the Lippizaner? Character is all-important during the arduous training of horse, and later of rider, and these greys have just the sterling qualities that are required. Standing some fifteen to sixteen hands, their nobility of nature is immediately apparent, even to a novice. Their alert, wide-eyed look, well-set ears and bearing of the head bespeak intelligence, and the muscled loins show strength and stamina.

Like every other animal, two or four-legged, the Lippizaner must be taught to become accustomed to discipline. The four-year-old horse must first undergo breaking-in. This is no bronco-busting, a five-minute job in a corral to the accompaniment of hat-waving and shouted encouragement from the crowd. No, indeed, the horses of this school are introduced to the rigours of control with kid-glove care. The actual breaking-in period alone takes two years!

The initial months are spent in lungeing work until the horse is developed enough to take a rider. Then the training continues under an expert horseman who sits completely passively on the animal's back. By talking to his mount and by small rewards for obedience, a confidence is slowly built up between rider and horse. After the initial period, a snaffle, the simplest and gentlest of bits, is used in place of the lungeing and side reins. Again confidence is built slowly and carefully over the next weeks; the horse is taken at slow paces, then at a trot, and finally the rider canters him around the ring, easing the corners as much as possible in order not to confuse his mount.

Later he is taught to obey the leg and the other signals; he is taught to halt properly, to turn in small circles, and in general to do all that a well-trained horse should accomplish in normal training.

From then on the horses graduate to the more exclusive manoeuvres: the Volte, tight turning, Passade, a turn on the haunches, Levade, Passage, Capriole, Piaffer, and so on — but only if they qualify over the first part of the long training course.

The Piaffer, a graceful 'marking time' by the horse, is taught in several stages. Firstly, by controlling the movements of the horse with a lungeing rein and whip, the riding master can shorten the stride of a trot, right down to the stage when the animal is actually trotting quietly on the spot without moving forward at all.

56

After learning the Piaffer 'on the Hand' the horse is sent to the pillars for further training.

In the centre of the ring at the Spanish Riding School stand two upright posts about four feet apart. In these the horse is loosely tethered and lessons in the Piaffer are continued, first without, and then with a passive rider. Soon the rhythm of the stationary trot becomes slower and more graceful, and finally the horse is allowed to perform without the aid of the pillars.

The Passage, the next stage in training, is merely a slowly forward-moving Piaffer, and is often seen performed by experts at the larger shows up and down Britain. It is one of the most majestic and beautiful movements to observe. Supported on alternating diagonals, a good stallion can perform a dignified, slow, regular manoeuvre that is a joy to watch.

From here the training progresses to the school canter, and preparation for the school springs. The Pirouette is mastered, the Mezair, with elevated forelegs, is learned, and later the Levade, Courbette and Capriole.

Both the Levade and the Capriole have often been the subject of great paintings, probably because they are most dramatic in appearance and have captured popular imagination.

In the Levade the horse balances on his hind legs; in the Courbette he hops with elevated forehand and deeply bent hocks — a movement once used in battle.

In the most spectacular of all, the Capriole, the horse springs high into the air; when his forehand reaches the highest point he kicks out horizontally with his hind legs, giving the appearance of a winged horse whose natural medium is the air. This is perhaps the most wonderful sight of all, a horse and rider sailing light as a feather through the air, several feet above the ground, all contact with earth left behind for a few moments of graceful, glorious flight.

The *Passade*

The most spectacular of all *haute école* movements, the *Capriole*

The Riders

The purpose of the Spanish Riding School of Vienna is threefold; its object, 'The conservation of the art of equitation in its most advanced stage', is achieved by public displays, by the training of horses, and by the teaching of pupils. Be those pupils completely inexperienced or 'born in the saddle', they all have to start again at the beginning at this school.

Training commences for the young pupils in the stables, where they work under the grooms, getting to know the animals and learning how to attend to them.

Then follows several months of lunge work on young horses. Pupils learn — or re-learn — to ride without reins or stirrups, acquiring the firm, balanced seat which is the basis of all good riding. Then for a while the horse is the instructor, as the students ride animals who have already been taught all the figures and movements of the school.

This is no short course. After a period which may last several years the pupil may be given a young horse of his own to train. If he is successful in this he is well on the way to becoming a *bereiter*, a riding-master.

Later, under the watchful eye of the Head of the School, he will be allowed to take part in the public appearances of the School . . .

As the riders enter the ring in their traditional uniform of black bicorn hat, buttoned-up tail coat, high collar and dazzling white breeches, as they doff their hats in eighteenth-century manner to the portrait of their founder, and commence their intricate show, what enthusiast could fail to be stirred by this wonderful establishment, steeped in classic tradition and staffed by riders who have devoted their lives to equestrian perfection?

And who could return home and not burn with a desire to improve his own prowess in this noble art, an art in which horse and man act in sympathy, harmony, and concert?

58

Right: A Horseguard on duty in Whitehall

A pair of greys drawing the State Coach at Princess Margaret's wedding

The mount of the State Drummer

The famous Blues of the Household Cavalry

THE PRINCE OF PALFREYS

The Dauphin: What a long night is this! I will not change my horse with any that treads but on four pasterns. *Ca, ha!* He bounds from the earth as if his entrails were hairs: *le cheval volant,* the Pagasus, *qui a les narines de feu!* When I bestride him, I soar, I am a hawk; he trots the air; the earth sings when he touches it; the basest horn of his hoof is more musical than the pipe of Hermes.

Duke of Orleans: He's of the colour of the nutmeg.

The Dauphin: And of the heat of the ginger. It is a beast for Perseus: he is pure air and fire; and the dull elements of earth and water never appear in him but only in patient stillness while his rider mounts him: he is indeed a horse; and all other jades you may call beasts.

Constable of France: Indeed, my lord, it is a most absolute and excellent horse.

The Dauphin: It is the prince of palfreys; his neigh is like the bidding of a monarch and his countenance enforces homage.

Shakespeare: Henry V, Act III, Scene 7.

HORSES IN
FABLE & FICTION

Paul Tabori
There are few animals, indeed, that have such intimate and ancient connections with literature as the horse. After all, where would poets and writers be without Pegasus, the Horse of the Fountain, that noble animal which sprang from the blood of Medusa when Perseus struck off the 'frightful Maiden's head'? Innumerable paintings and sculptures have celebrated the winged stallion, usually depicted in company with Bellerophon (who caught him with a golden bridle on the Acrocorinthus) and the goddess Athene, patroness of art, literature and philosophy.

The first horse, Greek mythology related, was created by Poseidon, the god of the sea. Erichthonius, the legendary first king of Athens, was the first to drive a chariot with four horses and was placed among the constellations as an *auriga* or charioteer. Far more sinister were the flesh-eating horses of Diomed, the tyrant of Thrace, which were fed on the strangers who were unlucky enough to visit the country. It was Hercules who finally overthrew the tyrant and, in poetic justice, fed Diomed's carcass to the horses.

Though Homer does not mention the story of the Wooden Horse of Troy in the Iliad, Virgil made the story immortal in his *Aeneid*. When Hector, the greatest Trojan hero, was slain, the wily Ulysses had a monster wooden horse built and spread the rumour to the Trojans that it was an offering to the gods to grant a prosperous voyage back to Greece for the beseiging army. The Trojans, rather foolishly and in spite of Cassandra's warnings, dragged the horse into their city. But, of course, it was full of Greek soldiers who slipped out at night, killed the Trojan guards, opened the gates and set fire to the great fortress city. This was the end of Troy — and the beginning of innumerable parallels being drawn between a wooden horse and any clever trick or military stratagem.

To the Greeks the chariot of Phoebus, the Sun-God, was drawn by a carefully selected team of horses. There was Actaeon (Effulgence), Aethon (Fiery Red), Amethea (No Loiterer), Bronte (Thunder), Erytheros (Red Producer), Lampos (Shining Like a Lamp), Phlegon (The Burning One, Noontide) and Purocis (Fiery Hot; also Noontide). But the god of the underworld, Pluto, also had his steeds — Abaster (Away from the Stars), Abatos (Inaccessible), Aeton (Swift as an Eagle) and Nonies; while Aurora, the Rose-Fingered Dawn Goddess, was drawn by Abraxas (a name which, curiously enough, was also used by the Gnostics for the Supreme Being), Eöos (Dawn) and Phoethon (the Shining One). The horse of

64

Bellerophon watering Pegasus, the winged horse. Roman relief, 1st century A.D.
Reproduced by kind permission of Alinari

Hercules was named Arion (Martial); created by Neptune, who brought it out of
the earth by striking the ground with his trident, it was a truly remarkable animal —
its feet were those of a man, it spoke with a human voice and ran with amazing
swiftness.

Neptune also gave a horse to Peleus which was later owned by Achilles. Its name
was Baios (Swift); its sire was the west wind and its dam Swift-foot, one of the
Harpies. The horse of King Adrastus, one of the Argonauts, was named Cerus (Fit)
and it was faster than the wind. Castor or Pollux (perhaps they shared it, as they
were such close friends) had a horse named Cyllaros; Diomed's was Dinos (The
Marvel), Hector owned one named Ethon (Fiery) and a second mount, Gala (The

65

The Wooden Horse of Troy, as constructed for the film *Helen of Troy*

Cream-Coloured). Neptune seemed to specialise in creating hybrid animals — his Hippocampus was a horse with only two fore legs, its hindquarters being those of a dragon or a fish. But perhaps the most human horse in the Greek epics was Xanthus, the Golden-Hued, who announced to his master Achilles his approaching death when the Greek hero unjustly scolded him.

It was a horse which, according to legend, won Darius the throne of Persia. When Smerdis died in 522 B.C., the rival candidates agreed that the king should be he whose horse neighed first when they met next day. The groom of Darius helped his master's chances a little by showing his horse a mare on the appointed place; as soon as the stallion reached the same spot the next day, it began to neigh and Darius became master of the kingdom.

Hercules on horseback. Italian bronze statuette, c. 1420—91. *Reproduced by kind permission of the Estense Museum, Modena*

In Moslem mythology, Al Borak, the miraculous horse that carried Mohamed from earth to the seventh heaven, had a respected place. This unique creature was milk-white, had the wings of an eagle, a human face, but the cheeks of a horse. It was of female sex and every step she took was equal to the extreme range of human sight. Her name was suited to this miraculous speed — for it meant 'lightning'. Mohamed's son-in-law, Ali, also had a famous horse, named Dhuldul. Guatama Buddha was usually described as riding Kantaka, his white palfrey. In Persian legend Ruksh, the hero Rustum's, horse was celebrated, and was immortalised by Matthew Arnold in his poem 'Sohrab and Rustum'.

Horses appear prominently in Nordic mythology as well. Grani, the 'grey-coloured', belonged to Siegfried, hero of the Nibelungenlied, and carried him with 'marvellous swiftness'. Hrimfaxi was the horse of Night in Scandinavian saga; from its bit fell the 'rime-drops' which every night bedewed the earth. Its companion was Skinfaxi, 'Shining Mane', the steed that drew the car of the day and is said to typify the wind that blows over land and water. In this hierarchy of horses Sleipnix was paramount — not only because he had eight legs and could traverse either land or sea but because his master was Odin himself.

The horse really came into its own with the great medieval romances, the chronicles of chivalry, the songs of minstrels. The very word 'chevalier' or 'cavalier' was rooted in the French 'cheval' and the Italian 'cavallo'. No knight could be magined without his trusted steed, no quest could take place without a mount. One could compile a vast list of the noble stallions and palfreys that prance and gallop across the pages of medieval literature — from King Arthur's stallion, Lamri, the Curveter, to Bajardo, in Ariosto's 'Orlando Furioso'. Bajardo was found by the wizard Malagigi in a cave guarded by a fierce dragon which the wizard had ito slay before he could take Bajardo away. This miraculous horse shares im-

67

mortality with Pegasus, for Ariosto tells us he is still alive — but when any man approaches he flees, so that no mortal can ever hope to catch him.

Bayard was also the name of the horse which the four sons of Aymon owned. They were the heroes of a medieval French romance, part of the great Charlemagne cycle, and they and their famous steed appeared in many poems and romances, including Tasso's *Jerusalem Delivered*, Pulci's *Morgante Maggiore*, Boiardo's *Orlando Innamorato* and Ariosto's *Orlando Furioso*. Bayard was a most accommodating horse — for he grew larger or smaller according to whether one or more of his masters wanted to mount him. His footprints are still shown in the forest of Soignes and on a rock near Dinant.

Equally famous was Bavieca, the horse of El Cid, the hero of Corneille's tragedy, the national hero of Spain and the great champion of Christianity against the Moors. Bavieca is the Spanish for 'simpleton' and the Cid's steed acquired its name because his master, as a youth, was given the choice of a horse and picked a rough colt instead of a fully-trained warhorse. His godfather called him a simpleton and the Cid promptly gave the name to his horse. After carrying him into innumerable battles and to countless victories, the horse survived his master by

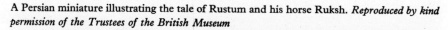

A Persian miniature illustrating the tale of Rustum and his horse Ruksh. *Reproduced by kind permission of the Trustees of the British Museum*

68

An old engraving of Bajardo, the horse which Orlando rode in 'Orlando Furioso'.

almost three years. No one was allowed to ride him and when he died he was buried outside the gate of a Valencia monastery with two elms to mark the site.

In Christian art the horse stood for courage and generosity and this, of course, was reflected in poetry and literature as well. The 'saints of chivalry', St Martin, St Maurice, St George and St Victor, were always represented on horseback, and the Quest for the Holy Grail would have been unthinkable without the 'noble animal' carrying the knights of the Round Table on their countless adventures, or bearing the Crusaders when they charged the infidel.

But though all these brave and faithful steeds were given names and the most desirable qualities a horse could possess, they were rather symbols and myths than living animals. It took the former galley-slave, roaming scholar and tax-collector, Miguel de Cervantes, to create a truly immortal horse in poor Rosinante. Cervantes was bent on giving the fading and phoney mystique of chivalry a death-blow — and wrote one of the greatest masterpieces of world literature. So much of *Don Quixote* has passed into the universal currency of mankind that Rosinante is only a companion to Dulcinea, Sancho Panza, the tilting at windmills and all the other enchanting creatures and incidents Cervantes gave us. Rosinante is a truly realistic animal — a wretched riding-horse, nothing but skin and bone, with a sagging back and swollen legs. In Spanish *rocin* means a jade and *ante* means 'before' — signifying that once upon a time Rosinante perhaps *had* been a horse. Yet to Don Quixote, the sad-faced knight of La Mancha, he was a priceless charger, surpassing 'the Bucephalus of Alexander and the Babieca of the Cid'. And if reality did not live up to the illusion — so much the worse for reality, Don Quixote declared. He came to grief again and again, on and off Rosinante — yet he never really forsook the ideals of true chivalry.

69

After Cervantes the horse in literature seems to acquire a split personality. One is still rooted in fable and mythology; the other is realistic, often satirical and pitiful. It would be easy to fill a tremendous gallery with portraits of horses representing both sorts. There was George Borrow's cob in *Lavengro* —

'. . . a tremendous creature! I had frequently seen him before and wondered at him; he was barely fifteen hands, but he had the girth of a metropolitan dray horse; his head was small in comparison with his immense neck, which curved down nobly to his wide back; his chest was broad and fine, and his shoulders models of symmetry and strength; he stood well and powerfully upon his legs, which were somewhat short. In a word, he was a gallant specimen of the genuine Irish cob, a species at one time not uncommon, but at the present day nearly extinct.'

One of the Christian 'saints of chivalry', 'Saint Martin and the Beggar', by El Greco. *Reproduced by kind permission of the National Gallery of Art, Washington, D. C. (Widener Collection)*

Borrow prided himself upon being a connoisseur of horse-flesh and whether it is *The Bible in Spain, Romany Rye* or *The Zincali*, you will find almost as many equine as human portraits in his books.

Borrow's was the expert's realistic approach; in a writer like Dostoievsky the horse often becomes a symbol of human suffering. There are moving descriptions of the horses that work at the convict camp in his brilliant *House of the Dead*. Gniedko, the bay horse 'a worthy sort of beast but a good deal worn', its successor, 'a capital gelding — young, vigorous and handsome, an irreproachable beast altogether' — these animals were petted, spoiled and provided a welcome diversion in the deadly monotony of prison life.

Contrast Gniedko, who never needed to be told where to go and when to wait for a load, with a rough steed in *The Three Musketeers* which D'Artagnan's father gave the young man when he set out for Paris. The plot really gets going when the young Gascon becomes involved in a brawl — because some men dare to laugh at his ungainly mount. Horses, usually anonymous, play a considerable part in the Dumas romances; they are sold and bought, diced away or received as gifts from generous high-born ladies, ridden to death on some desperate mission.

It is an equally anonymous horse that carries Ambrose Bierce's 'A Horseman in the Sky' to his death in this shattering Civil War tale, where a son has no choice but to shoot his father and see him plunge from a high cliff. The description is terse and graphic:

'... Lifting his eyes to the dizzy altitude of its summit, the officer saw an astonishing sight — a man on horseback riding down into the valley through the air! Straight upright sat the rider, in military fashion, with a firm seat in the saddle, a strong clutch upon the rein to hold his charger from too impetuous a plunge. From his bare head his long hair streamed upward, waving like a plume. His right hand was concealed in the cloud of the horse's lifted mane. The animal's body was as level as if every hoof-stroke encountered the resistant earth. Its motions were those of a wild gallop, but even as the officer looked they ceased, with all the legs thrown sharply forward as in the act of alighting from a leap. But this was a flight!'

Humourists, too, have given much attention to the horse — especially in connection with its unskilful or inexperienced rider. For several years the adventures of Mr Briggs, the honest merchant who aspired to social graces, were a feature of *Punch*. One could compile a whole anthology of *Punch*-horses behaving very unpleasantly to those who hire them for an hour or so — of Mr Briggs trudging back to the livery stables, dishevelled and out of temper; of steeplechasers refusing a fence; of the vagaries of horses when their masters are riding to hounds.

Paul Farkas, a witty Hungarian writer, devoted a whole book to the misadventures of young cadet-officers and their steeds, endowing his equine characters with almost fiendish ingenuity in causing trouble to their riders. And there is

Don Quixote on his wretched, but much-loved steed — Rosinante. *Reproduced by kind permission of the Mansell Collection*

a delightful story by the Austrian humourist Roda-Roda in which he described how a trickster who specialised in fleecing bishops and cavalry generals (according to him the two most gullible categories in the world) came to grief himself when posing as a major of the Hussars. He carried it off beautifully in the mess and at regimental headquarters — but unfortunately when it came to showing off his riding prowess, he attempted to mount the horse on the wrong side!

The racing stories which Nat Gold and his colleagues have written by the score (and are still writing) represent the popular literary 'appearance' of the horse. The formule is well-established and little varied: the big race, doped or sub-stituted favourites, the race-gang unmasked and brought to justice — these are the main elements. But some of these books have captured the atmosphere, and the excitement of racing. Here one should mention the eccentric and 'ornery' horses that crop up in P. G. Wodehouse's books, leading to disaster for his dimwitted heroes and presenting challenging tasks for his immortal Jeeves.

Horses have also been plentiful in children's stories — from Anna Sewell's *Black Beauty*, which has become a classic, to the 'Flicka' books, which Hollywood has turned into a series of films. *Black Beauty*, by the way, is one of the few books in which the horse-hero tells his own life; a plain unvarnished yet most attractive story, 'straight from the horse's mouth'. It must have inspired to a certain extent Enid Bagnold's *National Velvet*, a quite preposterous yet beautifully true novel in which a little girl rides her horse to victory in the Grand National. Almost as incredible as, yet a good deal more persuasive than, Munchhausen's famous horse which was cut into two by a cannonball yet went on galloping with the hero of the most uninhibited tall stories on his back.

72

Where the horse has not only come into its own but has become an indispensable character is in the perennial Western. From Zane Grey and Max Brand to the latest practitioner of the *genre*, the cowboy and his horse have been inseparable. The horses that thunder across the pages of *Riders of the Purple Sage* and the more than one hundred books of Grey, or are ridden by the cattle-rustlers and outlaws in Max Brand's countless books, are really symbols of the nostalgia for the American past. They have been transposed to the cinema and television screen in thousands of copies and have become part and parcel of American folklore, which the rest of the world has accepted and assimilated.

And the poets? Indeed, they have paid tribute to Pegasus and his descendants in thousands of verses. The 'milk-white steed' of Lady Margaret and the 'dapple-gray' of Lord William Douglas in the ancient ballad, the 'red-roan steed' in 'Edward, Edward', are passive actors in high tragedy. Bridles go 'jing-jingling' through the *Canterbury Tales* — the Knight, the Squire, the Monk, the Prioress, the Wife of Bath all have their distinctive mounts. And Shakespeare gives one of the most vivid descriptions of a proud stallion in 'Venus and Adonis', an extract from which is quoted elsewhere in this book.

Probably when Richard III uttered his famous (though quite unauthenticated) cry for 'A horse! a horse! My kingdom for a horse!' he would have been satisfied with a less perfect animal than that described in 'Venus and Adonis'.

Robert Burns's 'Elegy on Peg Nicholson' was a gentle epitaph for a humbler mount.

> 'Peg Nicholson was a good bay mare
>   As ever trod on airn;
> But now she's floating down the Nith,
>   And past the mouth o' Cairn.
>
> 'Peg Nicholson was a good bay mare,
>   And rode through thick and thin;
> But now she's floating down the Nith,
>   And wanting e'en the skin . . .'

Robert Browning's Roland who 'brought the good news from Ghent to Aix was no ordinary galloper:

> '. . . And his low head and crest, just one sharp ear bent back
> For my voice, and the other pricked out on his track;
> And one eye's black intelligence — ever that glance
> O'er its white edge at me, his own master, askance!
> And the thick heavy spume-flakes which aye and anon
> His fierce lips shook upwards in galloping on . . .'

The horse used in M-G-M's film of Enid Bagnold's *National Velvet*, which was ridden to victory by a little girl

Among the American poets the sensitive and musical Elizabeth Coatsworth has written a whole cycle of poems about horses; among these 'The Old Mare' has become a semi-classic. Other poets, before and since Walt Whitman, have sung in America about the horse. Louise Imogen Gurney in 'The Wild Ride'; Edwin Ford Piper in 'Sweetgrass Range'; H. H. Knibbs in 'Roll a Rock Down'; Amy Lovell in her exquisite 'Night Clouds'; Robert Frost in his gem-like 'The Runaway' and Mark Van Doren in 'The Distant Runners' — a sizeable anthology could be compiled of their poems.

But here I would like to end this brief survey of horses in fable and fiction with an extract from the Book of Job, which beautifully describes the majesty of this noble animal:

'Hast thou given the horse strength? Hast thou clothed his neck with thunder?
'Canst thou make him afraid as a grasshopper? the glory of his nostrils is terrible.
'He paweth in the valley, and rejoiceth in his strength: he goeth on to meet the
    armed men.
'He mocketh at fear and is not affrighted; neither turneth he back from
    the sword.
'The quiver rattleth against him, the glittering spear and the shield.
'He swalloweth the ground with fierceness and rage; neither believeth he that it is
    the sound of the trumpet.
'He saith among the trumpets, Ha, Ha; and he smelleth the battle far off, the
    thunder of the captains, and the shouting.'

74

Extract from

MAZEPPA

by Lord Byron

With flowing tail, and flying mane,
Wide nostrils never stretch'd by pain,
Mouths bloodless to the bit or rein,
And feet that iron never shod,
And flanks unscarr'd by spur or rod,
A thousand horse, the wild, the free,
Like waves that follow o'er the free,
Came thickly thundering on . . .
They stop, they start, they snuff the air,
Gallop a moment here and there,
Approach, retire, wheel round and round,
Then plunging back with sudden bound,
Headed by one black mighty steed,
Who seem'd the patriarch of his breed,
Without a single speck or hair
Of white upon his shaggy hide;
They snort, they foam, neigh, swerve aside,
And backward to the forest fly,
By instinct, from a human eye.

75

HORSES AND THE
CINEMA

Howard Loxton   When did the horse first appear in the cinema? The answer is that he has always been there. He was on the picture rolls of the zoetrope and the praxinoscope, the forerunners of the cinematograph. When children played with the newly invented zoetrope in 1833 they may have seen through the spinning slots a mounted cavalry man, dressed in his regiment's full regalia, continually trotting on and on; or perhaps they may have watched a pretty circus equestrienne cantering her horse round a never-ending ring and doing somersaults through a hoop.

The horse was there again at the next point in the cinema's history, when Eadward Muybridge, an Englishman living in California, took his first set of chronophotographs: a series of pictures recording the progression of a horse in motion.

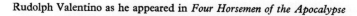

Rudolph Valentino as he appeared in *Four Horsemen of the Apocalypse*

Gene Autry and his horse Champion making their debut at the Savoy Hotel party

These were taken in 1877 to help Governor Sandford win a 25,000 dollar bet and prove that when a horse is galloping there is a moment when he has all four legs off the ground. Muybridge set up a battery of cameras each fitted with a string to set it off when the horse touched it; but the horse tried to jump over the strings, so he evolved a cylinder, like the one in a musical box, which, in turning, set off the cameras mechanically to match the horse's movement.

When the moving picture film eventually arrived in the 1880's most people thought of it as a nine-days'-wonder and directors made little films which did no more than show things that moved: people taking tea or leaving work, railway trains, and street scenes with horse-drawn cabs.

But the movie was here to stay, and in 1896 audiences in London stood on their seats and cheered when they saw the Derby on their screens and the Prince of Wales' horse Persimmon, the winner, go thundering past the finishing post.

The first real narrative film, made in America by Andrew Porter in 1903, was *The Great Train Robbery*. This told the story of a mail train hold-up and the pursuit and annihilation of the desperadoes. This short film was closely linked with the chases and gun fights of the touring 'Wild West' shows of the turn of the century, and set a fashion for 'Western' films which has lasted ever since.

In about 1906 film production in the U.S.A. moved from the eastern states to the more suitable film-making climate of sunny California. What these early film makers wanted was action, and in the western they had it — and in California they had ideal locations.

In the western tradition the horse is inseperable from his rider, whether cowboy, ranger or badman, not just as a means of transport, but as his rider's best and

Where would the Western be without horses?

closest friend; and as the human stars became more popular so did the horse stars as well. First of the cowboy stars was G. N. Anderson; but because film companies did not announce their actors' names (for fear that personal popularity might lead to demands for higher pay), his audiences knew him only as 'Bronco Billy'.

Next came 'Rio Jim' — or William Shakespeare Hart — and his piebald horse Fritz. Fritz once saved Hart's life. It happened when they were shooting a sequence at night, in which Hart and his cowboy band were to swim their horses across a turbulent mountain stream, lighting their way with burning torches. Hart went first and the swift water swept horse and rider into a whirlpool surrounded by an underwater slate ledge and a high wall. In vain they struggled to get out. Three times Fritz tried to climb the wall, only to fall back again. He tried to swim on to the ledge, but was swept away. At last Fritz fought back to the surface and, managing to get his forelegs over the ledge, he struggled out and pulled Hart with him.

Hart's usual role was that of a hard drinking, hard riding, hard shooting he-man. He was often an outlaw, often an enemy of law and order — but always true to the frontier's own moral code; a sort of 'good bad man' — not so far from life. But by the 1920's the public had decided they preferred a more romantic view of western life — now the hero became a 'good man', protecting the weak and on the side of the law. He did not drink and rarely smoked and only used his gun when he had to. He was clean and simple living. The stars who followed Hart and Fritz, of which the chief were Tom Mix and his horse Tony, belonged to an idealised west; and each new western built up the myth.

78

Right: A scene from the chariot race in M-G-M's *Ben Hur*

Relaxing in the spring sunshine

A Lippizaner stallion

Roping calves at a ranch in Arizona, U.S.A.

When sound came in 1927 and the movies began to talk, the cowboys learned to sing. Gene Autry rode and sang across the screen on Champion, and Roy Rogers made his first appearances with Trigger. There have been many clever horses who have learned their lessons well at drama school — there is a school in Hollywood that trains and teaches horses — but Roy Rogers claims for Trigger and his son, Trigger Junior, the title of the 'Smartest Horses in the Movies'. It is said that Trigger, a Palomino stallion, can walk 150 feet on his hind legs, sit on a chair, untie ropes, knock on doors, fire a gun, box and count up to ten, as well as perform old theatrical tricks like shamming a broken leg, pretending to be wounded and falling down dead. As a special personal touch he can also tuck his master up in bed! Trigger had his own contract with Republic Pictures, which guaranteed him billing as co-star and at least three close-ups in every film.

Roy Rogers on Trigger, one of the most highly trained film horses

The mounted cavalry officer, a common feature of the Western

Gene Autry's Champion also seems to be able to do everything but talk. As the finale of Gene Autry's touring show he dances the rhumba, waltzes, does the hula-hula and many other tricks, and then bows to thank the audience. Champion now has his own television series as 'Champion the Wonder Horse'. When he was appearing at the London Palladium he was the guest of honour at a party given in

A scene from *The Misfits*, in which wild horses are captured to be made into dog food

84

the Savoy Hotel, and once in Washington, D. C. he was ridden up the steps of the Capitol building to 'shake hands' with the President of the United States.

Life in the west is not always so romanticised in films today. In *The Misfits*, a film directed by John Huston with a scenario by Arthur Miller, we have a sort of anti-western. The whole film is heavy with Miller's symbolism. Its main characters see in the west an escape from an over-organised society with which they cannot come to terms. They make a living rounding up wild mustangs to be made into dog food. But in capturing the wild horses they are rounding up the only free things left and thus succeed in destroying what they wish to preserve. Huston presents the round-up of the mustangs in a splendid, but horrible, sequence, in which the terrified horses fight for their lives.

It is not only in the western that horses have made their mark. The cinema has gone to all sorts of periods and places for its plots and in many of them the horse plays an important part. The heart-throb of the silent screen, Rudolph Valentino in *Four Horsemen of the Apocalypse*, St Joan, Alexander, Ben Hur hurtling around the Circus Maximus, Sir Laurence Olivier as Henry V, the Teutonic Knights in

Laurence Olivier as Henry V, with the charger he rode in the film of *Henry V*

Eisenstein's *Alexander Nevsky* — all are accompanied by horses. And often in cinema spectacle the climax is a stampede, a cavalry charge, a tournament or a chariot race, for horses at speed provide an exciting, impressive sight.

But it is not only in films of vast size that the horse is so important. A favourite subject on a smaller, much more personal, scale has been the relationship between children and animals — and horses in particular.

Some have been based on original scenarios and some on well-known novels, such as *Black Beauty*, *National Velvet*, *The Red Pony* and *My Friend Flicka*.

One of the best films built around this relationship was a short French film entitled *Crin Blanc* (White Mane) made by Albert Lamorisse, which won the Grand Prix at the Cannes Film Festival and the Prix Vigo in 1953. Set in the salt, barren region of the Carmargue in the south of France, it is the story of a beautiful white stallion, leader of a herd, who loves freedom and hates men. He allows a small boy to capture and tame him, but when adults try to take the stallion from the boy, horse and boy swim out into the open sea — to the land in Carmargue myth

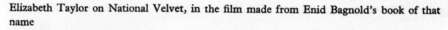

Elizabeth Taylor on National Velvet, in the film made from Enid Bagnold's book of that name

If there were an Oscar for horse actors, this decrepit Rosinante from the film *Don Quixote* would be a deserving winner

where horses can never be captured and a little boy and a stallion can live in peace and friendship for ever.

The Carmargue is the home of another film maker, Denys Colomb de Daunant, and among his several films about wild horses is *Un Sange des Chevaux Sauvage* (A Dream of Wild Horses), which uses the horses of the Carmargue to make a beautiful pattern of changing moods and forms. Filmed in slow motion, the horses' hooves splash in the waves and the salt spray slowly rises and slowly falls. They turn and move together, past, over each other, their manes flowing. This is a beautiful and poetic film, woven out of graceful movements of the horses, accompanied by an unusual, but very successful, sound track of *musique concrète*.

In the documentary field, horses are also featured in films about the land and agriculture. For instance, in the Hungarian film *Hortobagy* the horses play a most important part. In Alexander Dovzhenko's *Earth*, one of the world's great films, which deals with the collectivisation of the land and the superiority of the machine, the director most beautifully evokes our sympathy and love for the superceded horses.

What of the horse as an actor? Can one say that one horse plays his part better than another? The Triggers and the Champions are perhaps the most famous stars but as with human actors it is not always from the name in lights that the best performance comes. The character actors rarely get much public fame. What horse actor could face a greater challenge than that of Don Quixote's steed? In Gregori Kozintsev's version of Cervantes' famous classic, the horse gives a most excellent performance as Don Quixote's decrepit nag. If I had an Oscar to award I should give it to this splendid Rosinante.

87

Extract from

VENUS & ADONIS

by William Shakespeare

But lo, from forth a corpse that neighbours by,
A breeding jennet, lusty, young and proud,
Adonis' trampling courser doth espy,
And forth she rushes, snorts and neighs aloud:
The strong-neck'd steed, being tied unto a tree,
Breaketh his rein, and to her straight goes he.

Imperiously he leaps, he neighs, he bounds,
And now his woven girth he breaks asunder;
The bearing earth with his hard hoof he wounds,
Whose hollow womb resounds like heaven's thunder;
The iron bit he crushes 'tween his teeth
Controlling what he was controlled with.

His ears up-prick'd; his braided hanging mane
Upon his compass'd crest now stand on end;
His nostrils drink the air, and forth again,
As from a furnace, vapours doth he send:
    His eye, which scornfully glisters like fire,
    Shows his hot courage and his high desire.

Sometimes he trots, as if he told the steps,
With gentle majesty and modest pride;
Anon he rears upright, curvets and leaps,
As who should say, lo! thus my strength is tried;
    And this I do to captivate the eye
    Of the fair breeder that is standing by.

88

What recketh he his rider's angry stir,
His flattering 'holla', or his 'Stand, I say'?
What cares he now for curb, or pricking spur?
For rich caparisons, or trapping gay?
   He sees his love, and nothing else he sees,
   Nor nothing else with his proud sight agrees.

Look, when a painter would surpass the life,
In limning out a well-proportion'd steed,
His art with nature's workmanship at strife,
As if the dead the living should exceed;
   So did this horse excel a common one,
   In shape, in courage, colour, pace and bone.

Round-hoof'd, short-jointed, fetlocks shag and long,
Broad breast, full eye, small head and nostril wide,
High crest, short ears, straight legs, and passing strong,
Thin mane, thick tail, broad buttock, tender hide,
   Look what a horse should have, he did not lack,
   Save a proud rider on so proud a back.

Sometimes he scuds far off, and there he stares;
Anon he starts at stirring of a feather;
To bid the wind a base he now prepares,
And whe'r he run or fly, they knew not whether;
   For thro' his mane and tail the high wind sings,
   Fanning the hairs, who wave like feather'd wings.

He looks upon his love and neighs unto her;
She answers him as if she knew his mind:
Being proud, as females are, to see him woo her,
She puts on outward strangeness, seem unkind;
   Spurns at his love, and scorns the heat he feels,
   Beating his kind embracements with her heels.

Then, like a melancholy malecontent,
He vails his tail, that, like a falling plume,
Cool shadow to his melting buttock lent;
He stamps, and bites the poor flies in his fume:
   His love, perceiving how he is enrag'd,
   Grew kinder and his fury was assuag'd.

HORSES AT

WORK

Anthony Dent   It was many thousands of years before the horse ceased to be among the animals hunted for food, but became, with the dog, one of the two trusted servants of the hunters. Hunting ceased to be the sole gainful human activity, agriculture was invented and, after that, stock rearing. In turn, the ox, sheep, goat and pig were domesticated — we do not know quite in what order but all, certainly, before the horse.

When we do finally find the horse as a domestic animal, it is in the hands of the first two kinds of human specialists, the hunter and the warrior. What we know about the early domestication of the horse is derived inevitably from the early civilisations of Western Asia, because they alone have left written records which we can decipher. All of them show the horse as rarer and therefore more expensive than any other form of livestock. The law-code of an early Hittite king lays down prices thus:

Sheep	1 shekel
Goat	$\frac{2}{3}$ shekel
Cow	7 shekels
Horse (unbroken)	14 shekels
Ox (broken to plough)	15 shekels
Beef, ox or stud bull	10 shekels
Horse (broken to chariot)	20 shekels
Mule	60 shekels

Why should a mule cost three times as much as a horse? Partly, no doubt, because it was more difficult to produce, since, while the breeding of horses can be left to nature, mule-breeding, being the cross of a horse and a donkey, requires a certain element of human management. But probably also because the mule was more versatile; it could not only be yoked to the war chariot, but also to the wagon or the plough; it could be ridden and it could carry a pack-saddle.

Historical evidence shows that the use of horses in harness is more ancient than their use under the saddle. The earliest technical book about horses was written in about 1600 B.C. by Kikulli the Mittanite, who was in the service of a Hittite king. It is concerned solely with the training of chariot horses. The evidence of pictures also points to the same conclusion, since the earliest pictures of horse-

90

One of the first uses of horses was as pack animals. Here is an early picture of the clothmakers of England transporting their bales of cloth

drawn vehicles are far more ancient than the earliest pictures of ridden horses. In default of further evidence, it is accepted by archaeologists that driving is an invention of the Bronze Age while riding is an invention only of the Iron Age.

Research on the early stages of the use of horses by man is hampered by lack of archaeological evidence. Since there are no artifacts of stone associated with riding, the institution of riding has had to depend, for the archaeologist, on the survival of metal objects and of ancient pictures depicting riding. Admittedly it is almost impossible to conceive a metal-less civilisation that used horses in harness, but we have evidence in historic times of a culture that used the horse, for riding only, while it was without, or almost without, metal. The plains Indians of North America, when they rediscovered the wild horses that had escaped from the Spanish colonies, were at a more or less Neolithic stage of culture. They had no smelted metal of their own, a very limited amount of cold-hammered natural copper objects acquired from other tribes, and a still more limited amount of iron and brass 'trade goods' acquired from other tribes who were in contact with Europeans. They had absolutely no facilities for making metal bits, stirrups, girth-buckles or rivetted saddle-trees. Yet within a few generations, on a purely rawhide-and-wood basis, they reached a stage of equestrian culture comparable with that of the Scythians or the Cossacks.

Yet there is one employment for the horse probably older than either riding or driving, and that is as a pack-animal. The pack-train was the backbone of commercial transport in the Roman Empire. So it was in Europe throughout the Middle

91

Ages; inevitably so, since the medieval road-system everywhere in the west was the Roman road-system, worse and not better maintained than it had been in Roman times. Of course, the wagon and the cart also existed in the Middle Ages, but they seem to have been used for short rather than long journeys. Though it has practically vanished from Europe, the pack-horse still survives today in America, the most highly mechanised country in the world, where special conditions require its use among ranchers in the Rocky Mountain states.

In England, for a very long period, the ordinary word for a merchant, 'chapman', implied the owner of a string of pack-horses, and a particular breed of North-country pack-horse which developed into the Cleveland Bay was for long known as the Chapman Horse. Down to the late eighteenth century the bulk of traffic serving the great clothing industry was composed of pack-teams. The decline of the pack-horse as a commercial factor in Great Britain was rapid. In about 1830 the majority of pack-horses still operating were in the hands of small pedlars. But pack transport had once been big business: in the 1690's there was a regular goods service of pack-trains that ran to a timetable between Exeter and London.

In remote areas, like the Highlands of Scotland, the pack-horse held its own for much longer, as did other means of carriage by horse, but without wheels. Of these, the sledge is still in use on some hill-farms in the North of England for carrying hay and spreading muck. Earlier still the sledge had been used in the towns also, mainly for removing rubbish.

The use of horses in agriculture dates back to the Middle Ages, as can be seen from this illumination from the Luttrell Psalter

92

Today the horse is rapidly being superseded by the tractor, but he is still to be found on the farm in many parts of the world

The lack of a proper horse-collar was a severely limiting factor on the transport of the ancient world. For all their efficiency, the Romans had to rely on the clumsy yoke-and-strap system even for their heaviest vehicles. That is why even quite light chariots had to be drawn by four horses in the ancient world. But once a rigid horse collar had been evolved, little further development was necessary or possible. The same type of hill-and-trace harness seen in a fourteenth-century East Anglian miniature was still being made by London harness-makers in 1904.

The use of the wagon was not impossible without this gear (wagons were used by the Scythians and perhaps by all Indo-European nomads), but it alone permitted efficient horse traction. Wagons in antiquity were drawn either by oxen under the yoke, or disproportionately large teams of horses or mules. . . Since the ancient Scythians, Sarmatians and other steppe tribes appear to have possessed unlimited numbers of horses, wasted effort did not unduly worry them. But among our own Celtic and Saxon ancestors there were very few who could afford teams of more than four horses for one vehicle, and therefore the horses were more often put (usually in pairs) to the two-wheeled cart.

It was beyond the skill of any man, in any country, to build a wagon without metal parts, and the earliest users of wagons were probably the smiths themselves. Theirs was originally a nomadic calling, and the oldest driving bit in Great Britain was found in a cave above the Heathery Burn in Weardale, county Durham; this had been used as a temporary workshop by a family of wandering smiths in the Bronze Age. Nowadays, in the last age of the working horse, the shoeing smith has reverted to nomadic habits, since it is only the use of the mobile forge that enables the few surviving farriers of our day to get round their vast 'parishes'. The smithy,

And there are still a lot of odd jobs for a horse on the farm!

marked on pre-1914 Ordnance maps at about every other cross-roads, shows how recent was our dependence on the horse for local traffic, even after the railways had ousted it from the main roads.

Our image of the vast and powerful heavy breeds, for which Britain is famous, is of horses in the plough-team. But this, in fact, is a fairly recent development in the history of the horse. Like the wagon, the plough was originally drawn by oxen, for various reasons — sufficiently powerful horses had not been bred, oxen were more useful in providing flesh to eat, hides for clothing, etc., and there was a general reluctance to accept a change in farming practice. The replacement of plough oxen by horses began in the Middle Ages, but only in certain parts of England, and it was not complete by the end of the nineteenth century.

The experience of the Civil War had shown that the armour-carrying Great Horse was an anachronism on the battlefield dominated by musketeers and cannon; yet great numbers of heavy horses had been bred and imported by both factions for military use. If these great horses were not to be wasted, they must go to plough

An early form of transport for hay and straw, the sledge — still in use in the Yorkshire Dales

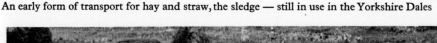

or work in draft, and there is no doubt that the enormous progress made in the second half of the seventeenth century both in long-distance land transport and in crop husbandry is due in the first place to this sudden surplus of heavy horses.

The wealth of new agricultural tools developed in the next age — rollers, drills, horse-rakes, reapers, mowing machines — were all designed to be drawn by heavy horses such as Shires, Suffolks, Clydesdales, and most of them have needed little modification to be equally useful behind the mechanical tractor. Such tools would have been quite useless to, say, the farmer of Charles I's day, because he did not have at his disposal a power unit equal to the Shire horse. Measurements carried out on the tractive power of draft horses in America have shown that a horse can develop 27 h. p.

But this development in the use of horses in agriculture does not mean that they played no part in earlier times. The four, six or eight ox team ploughed the land, but even in Anglo-Saxon times the horse harrowed in after them. The farmer sowed corn by hand, but the seed was brought to the field on a pack-horse. He reaped by hand also, but the sheaves were drawn back to the barn by horsepower. Every product of the farm that did not walk off the farm was carried away on or behind horses, and everything the farmer needed from outside came to him on or

The horse-drawn barge is a rare sight now on British waterways

The American Pony Express, operated in the 19th century, en route from the Missouri River to San Francisco

behind horses. Even such bulk cargoes as lime, sand and sea-ware and marl for manure were packed long distances in two-hundredweight horse-loads.

Without horses to get his produce to the market the farmer was powerless. He also needed a horse to get to the market himself, whether to buy or sell stock. Throughout the age of chivalry 'rouncies', or cobs, had been bred to carry the squire to war in support of the knight, but in the same period the same cobs carried tenants and bailiffs about their peaceful business, and for long after they remained the transport of all merchants and professional men.

All forms of practical administration required the services of mounted men, whether as active agents or as messengers. In the Roman Empire the backbone of the civil service, the curators and procurators, were the 'equestrian' officials perpetually touring their districts, and so it remained in the Middle Ages, when the central government itself progressed on horseback from London to Winchester, to Gloucester, to York, to London, while the King's justices journeyed on horseback from session to session.

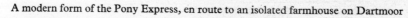

A modern form of the Pony Express, en route to an isolated farmhouse on Dartmoor

The stage-coach — gone for ever, but still revived for parades, like this handsome example

It was the same even in the world of learning. Oxford and Cambridge accounts of the seventeenth century regularly record purchases of saddle horses for the masters and Presidents of Colleges, the Manciples and their Stewards. In the early and austere days of English Christianity, even the much-debated stigma of wordly display could not prevent bishops, abbots and archdeacons from keeping horses essential in the course of their duties. The Jacobean Master of a college paid about £7 for a suitable horse, and the rural dean about the same.

Communication, too, was exclusively the province of the horseman, down to the beginnings of the semaphore in Napoleon's day. The history of the Royal Mail begins with horses, during the Empire of the Persians, who handed it down to the Chinese on the one hand, and on the other to the Romans via the Empire of Alexander the Macedonian.

Famous among mail services was the Pony Express, operated in America for a short time during the nineteenth century. Riders on horseback carried the mail, the horses being replaced at intervals of ten to fifteen miles; and very fast schedules were maintained in the face of great odds, including marauding Indians.

The industrial revolution in Britain, and in Western Europe generally, reached a fairly advanced stage without a system of land transport proportionate to its needs. But like the clothiers mentioned above, neither the ironmasters, nor potters and colliers could expand beyond a certain limit while their only means of transport in bulk were the pack-horse and the coasting ship. The first solution to this problem was the construction of canals, long before any mechanical means of locomotion had been devised. The beginning of the English inland waterway system

97

The horse tram was once a common feature of daily life, as this photograph of about 1888 shows. *Reproduced by kind permission of the Museum of British Transport*

dates from before 1750, and traction was provided by horses. Because of the complete lack of friction and initial inertia, a barge with a weight that could not be hauled by an eight-horse team on land could be moved by one horse. The chief requirements in a canal horse are steadiness and docility; speed is not desirable in canal traffic, since the waves set up tend to erode the banks.

Little is known, even by experts on canal lore, about the horsing of barges. But probably the barges were horsed largely from throw-outs from the studs of heavy horse breeders, as were the stage-wagons. The stage-wagon, for freight

But some people still use horse transport — gypsies, for instance

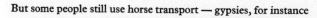

Arabs can carry a big man and a heavy stock saddle from dawn to dusk

The Whitbread 18th century dray

In many places horses are still an important part of agricultural life

Round-up of horses in California, U.S.A.

purposes, was only put out of business by the goods train, but it lost its passenger traffic some sixty years earlier to the stage coach, which was drawn by a very different class of animal and travelled to a much faster time-table. It cruised at a trot and often the team galloped for long spells, making an average of ten miles in the hour, which required bursts of nearly twenty miles per hour.

The operation of stage coaches soon became highly competitive and it is no wonder that the maximum working life of a horse in this traffic was about four years. A very superior class of horse was required for this work by about 1820, but of course contractors could not afford to pay top prices (to run a regular service of four-horse coaches required one horse per mile of road), so that almost every stage-coach horse had some fault which debarred it from private use, either of conformation, soundness or temperament. Four-horse teams with only two eyes between them were not unknown. Kickers were commonplace, as was partial lameness. The stage-coach, and its successor the mail-coach, had a short day, but nevertheless the literature of the mail-coach is enormous, since as a spectacle it was unique in its age.

The horse is still irreplaceable in the service of law and order. It had been the custom on the continent to enforce unpopular measures on unwilling taxpayers by quartering dragoons among them, and this method was adopted in Great Britain.

And these Navajo Indians from a reservation in New Mexico, who still preserve their nomadic customs

Dragoons were also employed against smugglers in Britain. The first paid constabulary in London, the famous Bow Street Runners of the late eighteenth century, ,were largely Bow Street Riders — they had to be in order to counter the mounted highwaymen.

The control of crowds, especially crowds assembled with political aims, was at first no business of the constabulary, but of the 'military', first of regular dragoons and later of volunteer yeomanry. The county regiments of yeomanry did not go on active service until the South African wars, but at home they were called out many times in aid of the civil power. Only gradually was this function taken over by a mounted arm of the civil police, first in London. The metropolitan force, because of its great success in peaceful crowd control, was soon imitated in the larger cities of Great Britain, and finally in almost every major capital of the world. The London police horse nowadays works a four-hour day, with a period of service of twelve years. It is unlikely to be supplanted in the forseeable future, since there are certain functions which it can perform better than all the jeeps and tommy-guns and gas grenades in the world.

Probably, therefore, the police horse will be the last of its species to disappear from the urban scene, which it dominated as late as 1914. The railways brought more people and more goods to the cites, but for almost a century passengers and goods alike had to be carried from station to final destination behind horses. Both the tram and the omnibus were first powered by horses, and even the railway was

In the open spaces of New South Wales, Australia, horses are still indispensable to the sheep farmer. *Reproduced by kind permission of the Australian News and Information Bureau*

And the cattle rancher of the Northern Territory
still rounds up his cattle on horseback

first intended for horse traction. But late inventions rapidly superceded the horse
in these spheres.

The use of horses was realised very early in the history of stock-rearing. The
first domestic cattle of Europe were descended from the great wild ox, which

In the Canadian West, too, the horse is the only means of transport for this kind of job

For some police work, the horse has not yet been, and perhaps never will be superseded by machines

was a huge, powerful and rather fast-moving beast, practically impossible to herd on foot. In Britain it was largely replaced in early times by the Celtic Shorthorn, a smaller and much more docile beast; but in the Western Mediterranean, the descendants of the wild ox still run on the plains and plateaus, in the form of the Camargue cattle of France and the black fighting bulls of Spain. Today, as from time immemorial, they are herded by mounted men, and it is from these men and their traditions that the gaucho and vaquero of Latin America, the cowboy of the West United States and the stockman of the Australian and New Zealand ranges derive.

They need not now be so numerous, so daring, or quite so inured to hardship as their forebears, because the original vaqueros herded their stock on unfenced pasture as in Bronze-Age Europe. The modern cowboy or stock-hand is largely occupied in patrolling wire fences round paddocks with a perimeter of dozens of miles. But still his skill in horsemanship is needed in driving and cutting out cattle at all seasons of the year.

Police horses putting their arduous training into practice, against crowds in London

106

RODEOS

Douglas Eastwood

'Rodeo' is Spanish for roundup. And originally rodeos were simply country fairs designed as exhibitions of cowboy skill at riding and handling ranch stock. Nowadays, rodeos are Big Business. Each year in America alone, more than ten million spectators pay for admission to rodeo shows.

Many of the men who ride the wild rodeo broncos are professionals, moving around the country from show to show and earning good money. Occasionally, however, one finds a rodeo from which professional riders are barred — such as that at Stamford, Texas. Nevertheless the men who make their living at bronco riding have plenty of scope; the United States alone has about 250 rodeos each year. Rodeos are held, too, in Canada, Australia and occasionally in Europe.

Rodeos first became a part of show business in 1888, when people first paid cash to watch bronco busting at Prescott, Arizona. Before this, riders had worked simply for the love of it, and to demonstrate their skill to neighbours. In the early days, rodeos were confined to ranching areas. Now you can find them in every part of the United States. Each September at Madison Square Garden, New York, is held the biggest show of all — the World Championship Rodeo. Huge prizes are offered, and won by the star riders of the rodeo world.

There is nothing gentle in the bronco riding exhibitions to be seen at rodeos. Although the official time allotted to each bout between horse and man is only ten seconds, a great deal happens in that short space. The bucks and twists used by the horse to unseat his rider are known by various technical terms, such as sidewinders, sunfishers and piledrivers. Most of the broncos used at rodeos are as professional as the riders themselves, with enormous repertoires of wicked tricks.

Some of the horses are ridden bareback; these animals wear a surcingle or belt around the belly, with two leather loops attached. The rider is permitted to hold only one of these loops, and he must not change hands during the ten seconds. Incidentally, an experienced bronco can buck about thirty times in the space of ten seconds. In 'saddle bronco riding' the horseman has strict rules to observe: he is not allowed to wrap the rein around his hand; he is not allowed to grab the saddle; the hand not holding the rein must be held aloft during the contest; and while he is mounted he must continually 'rake' the horse's flanks with his heels.

About a hundred years ago, Europe had a taste of the Wild West when the Buffalo Bill show arrived from the United States. In Italy, the show's bronco busters received a challenge from an Italian nobleman, the Duke of Sermonata. The Duke had a group of ferocious horses which Italian riders had tried in vain to tame. Would Buffalo Bill's riders care to try? According to the *New York Herald* the challenge was accepted. Before an audience of twenty thousand spectators the cowboys caught, tamed and rode the savage horses within five minutes.

Buffalo Bill's English rival in the world of show business, Lord George Sanger, decided to add a Wild West exhibition to his circus. At Liverpool in 1854 he staged a show of buck-jumping horses. His method of training them was simple. He pricked the animal on the withers with a pin, causing it to rear. This was done several times, until finally the pin was discarded and the animal reared at the touch of a finger. To make the horse fling up his hindquarters the pin was jabbed into the crupper. Rather an odd method of training for a man reputed to be an ardent lover of animals.

A bronco has an enormous repertoire of wicked tricks — like this one!

But this cowboy looks as if he's ready for them

Horsemanship other than bronco busting is to be seen at the modern rodeo. 'Roman riding' is popular. In this, the rider stands on two horses abreast, a foot on the rump of each animal. Sometimes races are held between riders straddling horses in this fashion, the men frequently urging their mounts over hurdles while retaining a foothold on their backs. Jimmy Murphy, a star of the rodeo arena, rides a pair of white stallions through a flaming hoop. Well known at America's rodeos is Nancy Sheppard. As pretty as she is daring, Miss Sheppard works while her horse is at full gallop; her tricks include hanging by one foot from the saddle in Cossack style, and manipulating lariats while performing a saddle-stand at top speed. Miss Sheppard's mount is a sturdy piebald with the steady gait so essential to this type of work.

Many people believe that the horses used in rodeo bronco-busting exhibitions are unbroken wild horses. This is not so. Most of the animals are horses with a 'mean streak' which have been found too savage for domestic work. Horses can and do become savage through rough handling. Incorrect gelding, too, can turn a normally docile horse into an outlaw. Many of the rodeo horses have such a hate of carrying a rider that they will go to any lengths to rid themselves of him. Now and then you will find a 'killer' horse who will not hesitate, if all else fails, to stand on his hind legs and topple over backwards, pinning the cowboy beneath him. Many of the professional rodeo riders wear leather belts under their clothes to protect them from internal injury. Bronco riding is a one-sided affair: although it is 'no holds barred' so far as the horse is concerned, the rider must strictly adhere to the rules enforced by the Rodeo Cowboy Association.

The Calgary Stampede is one of the biggest and best known rodeos. Held in Alberta, Canada, it lasts a week and takes place annually. Events include not only the riding of bucking horses but races between four-horse teams attached to wagons, musical chairs on horseback, wild cow milking contests, whip cracking and roping from galloping horses.

Points in bronco riding are awarded to riders who manage to stay on the horse's back for the standard ten seconds; points also go to the rider's style and his observation of the rules. Although rodeo riders are not paid a regular salary, they can make large amounts of money if they possess the necessary riding skill.

Horses, of course, are the main attraction at any rodeo. Apart from the bucking broncos, the 'bad boys' of the horse world, there are the clever ponies used by the cowhands in rounding up stock, and the trained mounts of the trick riders. Cutting individual calves from a herd of cattle is one of the jobs of the ranch-horse usually seen at rodeos. Incredible though it may sound, horses (including Arabians) have been trained to perform this kind of work *without a rider*, cutting out calves from the herd at the verbal command of the cowboy. We take it for granted to see a sheepdog doing this kind of thing; to teach a horse such work requires endless patience and knowledge of equine psychology.

Roping calves is a popular Rodeo event

Although occasionally horses are injured at rodeos, particularly in the bronco riding contests, the buck-jumpers on the whole have a fairly easy life. They work for only ten seconds at a time, about twenty times a year. Sometimes you will find a killer bronco who 'turns soft' for no apparent reason and is sold from the rodeo string to work much harder elsewhere. Which seems to prove that, for rodeo horses anyway, crime certainly *does* pay.

Lassooing a moving horse, like this, demands a high degree of skill

HORSES IN

WAR

Paul Tabori   Archaeologists and palaeontologists have proved that man's stature has grown steadily throughout the ages. The armour of the Middle Ages preserved in museums proves that most of the valiant knights were rather short. And just as the centuries have put inches on Average Man, horses have also increased in size. That is why the war-horses of ancient Egypt, India and Assyria were never ridden. They were too small to carry an armed man — and were only used to draw chariots. Chariots needed level surfaces or roads, so they were not much use in any battle over rough ground.

The first proper cavalrymen were probably Nubians; Egyptian reliefs show them riding horses that were taller and more powerful than anything seen before. This breed is said to have come from the district of Dongola, and the strain still survives in the Sudan. They were the ancestors of the Arabian horses and spread gradually into Europe.

Xenophon, the Greek general and historian, was the first to provide detailed instructions for the training and command of a squadron of horsemen; yet in ancient Greece the horses were still too small and too few to be used against the

Horses were used in warfare in pre-Christian times. These are cavalry of the Macedonian Army

A complete war harness for man and horse of c. 1475—85, from the castle of Hohenaschau in Upper Bavaria. *Reproduced by kind permission of the Trustees of the Wallace Collection*

heavily armed and perfectly disciplined foot-soldiers, the *hoplites*. Cavalry was used less for fighting than for reconnaissance.

The Romans were forced to develop armour against the barbarian tribes; but the more protection a mounted soldier needed against stones and arrows, the heavier he became. The heavy cavalry was too heavy in the end to gallop; and the light cavalry was not good enough for any massed charge. Thus the lighter and better mounted tribesmen of Asia, who erupted into Europe under Attila, the Hun, and other leaders, found their task easy. They were highly mobile, carried their food under their saddles and could make lightning forays, laying waste whole districts, avoiding fortresses and strong points. The Huns, and later the Magyars, became the terror of early medieval Europe, appearing unexpectedly in the most unlikely places, looting and burning and then disappearing with equal suddenness.

As chivalry developed, the knight became sheathed in more and more armour and this led to the breeding of huge horses that could carry immense weights. But they were extremely expensive and only the wealthy could afford them. Nor

113

19th century Austrian cavalry

were these masses of steel and iron effective against eight or ten ranks of disci-plined foot-soldiers armed with eighteen-foot pikes. Towards the close of the fif-teenth century infantry remained masters of the battlefields of Europe.

The change came with the invention of gunpowder and firearms. Pistols, unlike crossbows and longbows, could easily be fired from the saddle; gradually the knights and their retainers (who could afford the new weapons) provided them-selves with long pistols in addition to their lances and swords. Bullets could pierce any armour a foot-soldier could carry.

The French were the first to introduce the new tactics, at the battle of Cerisoles in 1544, against the English. A squadron of cavalry, formed of from twelve to sixteen ranks, trotted up to within pistol shot of the square of foot-soldiers to be attacked; then each rank cantered off man by man to the left, discharging his pistol at the square as he passed and wheeling back to his place behind the column to reload. Against the new tactics infantry was helpless; nor did the stakes help which the English archers carried to check any direct cavalry charge. The *chevaux de frise*, the ancestor of barbed wire, was also of little use, though the Austrians continued to use it against the swift charges of Turkish cavalry till the end of the seventeenth century.

The counter-tactics were evolved finally in Bohemia, Moravia and Poland, where great trains of wagons, accompanied by infantry, were set up in as many as twelve parallel lines to form *laagers* (as copied by the Boers almost five hundred years later) against which the cavalry battered in vain. Wagon-fortresses became the equipment of every European army and by the close of the sixteenth century the three main branches of artillery, cavalry and infantry were clearly developed. Two of these, of course, depended on horses.

The two great cavalry leaders of the Reformation were the Swedish king Gus-tavus Adolphus, whose strongly disciplined horsemen could be relied on not to throw away victory for the sake of looting the enemy's baggage, and Oliver Crom-well, whose mounted Roundheads were more than a match for the Cavaliers.

In the Flanders campaigns of the late seventeenth and early eighteenth century cavalry rapidly degenerated into mounted infantry; swords and lance-proof armour were abandoned for long muskets and heavy ammunition. The division into heavy, medium and dragoons for the cavalry had taken place some time before; and generals like Marlborough — or 'Corporal John', as his soldiers called him — knew how to employ the different formations to the best effect.

When Frederick the Great ascended the throne, his cavalry was pretty bad. 'They can manoeuvre,' the Prussian king said, 'with the same precision as my grenadiers but unfortunately they are equally slow.' Frederick's enemies, the Austrians, could boast of the dashing Hungarian Hussars (it was a troop of Hussars that once made a lightning sortie right to Berlin; their purpose, as their commander Hadik explained, was 'to get some gloves for the Empres', Maria Theresa) and at battles like Mollwitz the Prussians escaped disaster only by the rapidity of their infantry fire. But three years later Frederick had completely reorganised his cavalry and at Hohenfriedberg the Bayreuth dragoons, with 1,500 horses, dispersed 20 Austrian battalions, took 2,500 prisoners and captured 67 flags.

It was Prussian cavalry which defeated the French army at Rossbach, and General von Seydlitz, who commanded, saved the day for the Prussians with his perfectly trained horsemen at Zorndorf the next year by destroying the Russian right wing and centre. When Seydlitz died at the age of 52, his brilliant forces declined and the French cavalry took the lead. They evolved the three main types that remained in being up to the First World War: the cuirassiers, who rode the best big horses for heavy charges, the hussars, with the best light horses, and finally the dragoons, who were in reality just infantry on horseback and had the remaining mounts. The Austrians, having learned nothing from the lessons of the Seven Years' War, became even less effective than the Prussians — or, for that matter, the

A parade of Polish cavalry of 1932. *Reproduced by kind permission of the Polish Cultural Institute*

British, whose traditional style of horsemanship made it extremely difficult to train them for combined and disciplined action.

Up to the campaign of Poland, Napoleon only used his cavalry for reconnaissance and (as at Jena) for completing the destruction of a beaten enemy by pursuit. But after the terrible losses in 1806—7, the Emperor introduced new tactics. His artillery, using case-shot, sowed confusion and fear in the enemy's ranks; then masses of cavalry led the attack, overwhelming the foe by sheer weight of men and horses. At Waterloo this method failed — the ground was too heavy, the slope was against the charge and the horses were not in good enough condition for the task demanded of them.

So did the charge of the Light Brigade fail, although truly deserving the exclamation of the French general: '*C'est magnifique mais ce n'est pas la guerre.*' The six hundred who rode down 'into the Valley of Death' were sent to their doom by a mistaken command, and while their courage was justly celebrated by Tennyson and their fellow countrymen, by the time of the Crimean War cavalry had practically ceased to exist in most armies. Nor did the great exploits of both Northern and Southern cavalrymen in the War between the States stop this decline. There were magnificent raids and amazing feats of bravery in the Civil War by mounted men — but in the end the conflict was decided in favour of the industrial capacity and the better-trained infantry of the forces of Lincoln.

In the Boer War, British cavalry proved inferior to the fast and tenacious Boer horsemen — though the war was over before such Boer generals as de Wet and de la Rey could develop the cavalry tactics of shock and cold steel. And by the time the First World War burst upon the world, some military strategists argued that only artillery and infantry should be employed. Yet the horse still continued to play an important part in the world-wide conflict — expecially on the Eastern front, where Cossacks and the 'Red Devils', the Hungarian Hussars, clashed repeatedly in pure cavalry charges.

In the West, however, as soon as trench warfare froze the frontlines into positions which did not change materially from the autumn of 1914 to the summer of 1918,

German Uhlans going into action in the 1914-18 war

A British Army encampment at Suvla Beach during the Dardanelles Campaign of 1915.
Reproduced by kind permission of the Imperial War Museum

cavalrymen were quickly dismounted. Horses were employed as beasts of burden and many thousands of them perished in the mud of Flanders and Eastern France. The machine gun and the long range, quick-firing, heavy artillery had made any frontal attack on horseback impossible. In minor sectors — such as Africa, Manchuria or the Balkans — mounted soldiers were still employed on limited reconnaissance missions but the days of the massed, thrilling cavalry charges were gone for ever.

The only country that did not seem to have learned this lesson between the two great wars was Poland. Or perhaps she had no choice; her poverty and misgovernment did not allow proper mechanisation of her armed forces. In the tragic days of September 1939, Polish cavalry — the best-trained and most daring in the modern world — was hurled against the German tanks and was decimated and destroyed in a vain attempt to stem the invasion.

Generally speaking, the horse played a very small part in the Second World War. During the winter campaigns in Russia there were some Cossack units which were used for reconnaissance over the snowy wastes or for rounding up isolated German remnants. The Japanese, too, used cavalry in China and Manchuria for similar purposes. But the great days of warhorses, of flashing sabres and blood-curdling battlecries had ended more than a century before.

Yet the glory of some individual horses lives in history. Alexander the Great's Bucephalus, who would never carry any other rider and knelt down to take up his master, was honoured at his death (he lived to the ripe age of thirty) by a city being built as his mausoleum, called Bucephalia. Wellington's Copenhagen, the charger he rode at Waterloo, lived to twenty-seven; the remains of Marengo, the white stallion which Napoleon mounted at the same battle, are still preserved in the United Seervices Museum, London.

117

Mr Jorrock's Advice on
WHAT TO LOOK FOR
IN A HORSE

The height of an 'oss, Gambado says, is perfectly immaterial, prowided he is higher behind than before. Nothin' is more pleasin' to a traveller than the sensation of continually gettin' forward; whereas the ridin' of an 'oss of a contrary make is like swarmin' the bannisters of a staircase, when, though you really advance, you feel as if you were goin' backwards.

Gambado says nothin' about the size of an 'oss's head, but he says he should carry it low, that he may have an eye to the ground and see the better where he steps. Some say the 'ead should be as large as possible, inasmuch as the weight tends to prewent the 'oss from rearin', which is a vice dangerous in the highest degree; my idea is, that the size of the 'ead is immaterial, for the 'oss does't go on it, at least he didn't ought to do, I know . . .

A long back is a grand thing for a family 'oss. I've seen my cousin Joe clap six of his brats and his light porter on the back of the old Crockerdile, and the old nag would have carried another if his tail had been tied up. In the 'unting field, however, one seldom sees more than one man on an 'oss, at a time. *Two* don't look sportin', and the world's governed by appearances.

Some people object to high blowers, that is 'osses wot make a noise like steam engines as they go. I don't see no great objection to them myself, and I think the use they are of clearin' the way in crowded thoroughfares, and the protection they afford in dark nights by prewentin' people ridin' against you, more than counterbalance any disconwenience. Gambado says, a bald face, wall eyes and white legs answer the same purpose, but if you can get all four, so much the better.

There is an author who says the hip-bones should project well beyond the ribs, which form will be found werry conwenient in 'ot weather, as the rider may hang his hat on them occasionally, whilst he wipes the perspiration from his brow, addin' that that form gives the hanimal greater facility in passin' through stable doors; but I am inclined to think that the advice is a little of what the French call *pleasantre* and we call gammon; at all events, don't follow it.

Handley Cross (R. S. Surtees)

118

The Tower Circus, Blackpool

A charming study of a mare and foal

Youngster from the National Stud

FAMOUS HORSES IN

Peter Roberts

Today many horses are famous in their own right. In sport, particularly, the names that are written into the lists of winners are those of the mount, not the rider.

This was not always so. In the Middle Ages the horse was regarded solely as another instrument of labour, a vehicle of work, and any that have been mentioned in the chronicles of the historians of that date have had to thank the man who rode them for their immortality.

King John — who was not always as bad as he was painted — altered the 'public image' of the horse when he imported a hundred Flemish stallions for breeding. He set a trend which was followed by other monarchs, notably King Edward the Third, who shipped over a number of Spanish horses to improve the strain here in Britain. Later King Henry the Eighth laid down strict rules for the interbreeding of British horses, presumably with an eye to bigger and better cavalry mounts. Thus the horse became the first status symbol. But there were one or two horses that secured their niche in history long before these events . . .

Bucephalus was a superb stallion bred in the lush pastures of Thessaly in the fourth century B.C. Coal black apart from the white star on his forehead, Bucephalus was brought to the attention of Philip II, then King of Macedonia. A great horse lover, Philip bought the horse on first sight for the equivalent of £6,000. It seemed a bad buy, for Bucephalus proved uncontrollable, the king's horsemen being unable to cope with the fiery stallion. According to the story, King Philip's twelve-year-old son Alexander then stepped forward and begged his father to let him try and master the stallion. His father reluctantly agreed. Alexander was only a young stripling, but he had noticed that Bucephalus was frightened of his own shadow and took steps to see that the stallion avoided casting a shadow in front while he rode him.

Soon Bucephalus accepted the rider and became completely docile, to the delight of the King, who broke down with joy on seeing the skill his son showed with the horse. How much of this is true? One can only guess, but it is known that the young Alexander became 'the Great' and Bucephalus was his favourite charger.

Bucephalus accompanied Alexander the Great on all his campaigns, and when his horse had passed his prime, Alexander would ride other mounts for such tasks as reviewing his troops and only use Bucephalus to carry him into battle.

123

Left: H. M. the Queen on 'Winston' at the Trooping of the Colour Ceremony

Eventually Bucephalus died in action beneath his master from arrow wounds in the neck. So ended one of the first friendships between horse and master.

Incitatus was one of the first racehorses, whose story is as colourful as that of his owner. Incitatus was owned by the Roman Emperor Caligula (A.D.12 to A.D. 41), an emperor who became known for his brutality towards the end of his life. But the brutality of which he was undoubtedly guilty was never directed against his horses. Quite the reverse in fact, for whenever Incitatus was due to race, he was assured a restful sleep the night before the race. Caligula made sure of this by posting his soldiers throughout the neighbourhood to ensure silence.

Incitatus was rewarded after his victories with honours unmatched even today. Emperor Caligula gave his horse a private house, staffed with slaves whose task it was to see to his comfort, and furnished with an ivory manger, marble bedrooms and gold feeding buckets.

The wins of Incitatus aroused little enthusiasm in the hearts of Caligula's courtiers, for a victory meant that they had to dine with the horse, and none dared refuse. Later the Emperor ran out of honours, and made Incitatus first a full citizen, then a senator! The fate of the victorious Incitatus is not known, but he probably retired with the smug satisfaction of being the first horse in the world to enter politics.

El Morzillo can also claim an equine 'first' — that of the first horse to become a god. In the sixteenth century, Cortes sailed from Cuba to capture Mexico, and later wrote, 'after God, I owe the victory to the Horses'. Yet his cavalry consisted of only sixteen horses!

The reason for the success of the horse in Cortes' battle was that the Indians had never seen such an animal before and looked upon the rider and animal as being one beast and quite naturally fled from it.

Of these sixteen, the greatest was El Morzillo, or the 'Black One', Cortes' favourite charger.

Six years later, Cortes was again riding El Morzillo, in an expedition south to Honduras, this time with a cavalry of ninety horses. On the way El Morzillo got a splinter in one of his forefeet. For the sake of the expedition, Cortes reluctantly left his faithful horse with a friendly Indian chief, but noted in his diary that he doubted if he would ever see El Morzillo alive again. He was right.

The Indians did all they could for the horse, but El Morzillo soon died. In an effort to lessen the revenge the Indians feared Cortes would take, they built a statue of the horse to offer to Cortes when he returned. Cortes never did come back, but the beauty of El Morzillo had had a great effect on the Indians and soon they were worshipping the statue. El Morzillo had become a god.

For 170 years, the statue of El Morzillo ruled the district, and it was only the intervention of Franciscan monks which prevented the cult from spreading. They destroyed the sculpture and with it the legend of the god-horse.

124

Alexander the Great, who owned the fiery stallion Bucephalus. *Reproduced by kind permission of the Trustees of the British Museum*

Marocco was a horse that proved a novelty in the Elizabethan age when novelties and eccentricities abounded. For Marocco was a performing horse, one of the first on record.

Described at the time as 'a middle-sized bay gelding of fine conformation', Marocco, the dancing horse, came from Newmarket, which even in the days of Queen Elizabeth was already a centre for the horse in Britain. Marocco was owned by Thomas Bankes, a Scot, whose training of the horse must have been as good as the intelligence of Marocco himself, for it was reliably reported at the time that Marocco could perform the *haute école* movements with no trouble, dance a Tudor jig, popular at the time, walk on his hind legs and even move backwards in small circles while in that upright position.

125

Bankes made good use of the horse and it was often to be seen performing at the Belle Sauvage Inn at Ludgate Hill, London, where it could rap out the numbers turned up by dice players, return a pair of gloves to the correct owner and tell the number of pence in a silver coin. According to equestrian experts at the time, Marocco was considered a horse of exceptional intelligence, but it was thought that many of the tricks relied on the showmanship of Bankes.

However, the tricks were sufficiently well presented to convince Tudor London that it was done with black magic. The success in the end proved the downfall of Bankes and a tragic ending for Marocco.

In the case of *Black Bess* the task of separating the legend from fact is more difficult than for any other horse in history.

This state of affairs was both helped and hindered by Harrison Ainsworth when he published his novel *Rookwood*, for in the closing chapters of this book Turpin's famous ride to York on Black Bess is described down to the last quivering gasp. Though both Turpin and Black Bess did exist, the ride did not, and Ainsworth is largely responsible for the myth. Oddly enough, though, Ainsworth must also be thanked for what we do know about the man and the horse, for he did a good deal of research into their stories before his novel appeared.

The ride in *Rookwood* was actually based on that of another highwayman — John Nevison, who was born in 1639 and who became a highway robber of the stamp of the Dick Turpin of the storybooks. About 1676, Nevison staged a robbery near Rochester, and fearing he was recognised decided to make the ride to York to establish an alibi. He set off in the early hours of the morning, completed the ride of 231 miles in sixteen hours, and was seen playing bowls with the Lord Mayor of York that evening. Though the stirring tale is true, the most important piece of information is left out — that is, the number of horses he used for the journey. For all his efforts, Nevison was arrested and only saved from the gallows by King Charles II, who pardoned such a sporting rogue.

Richard Turpin was unfortunately not of the same ilk, but this has never hampered the historian. Turpin was more like the Roman Emperor Caligula — a brutal man when it came to dealing with his fellows, but a man devoted to his horse to the extent of being called an eccentric.

It would be pointless to attempt to describe Black Bess, for there would be little hope of authenticity. Turpin was authentic, though, as many wealthy travellers found to their cost. While attempting to steal a racehorse called 'White Stockings', Dick Turpin and a man called King were caught red-handed and during a fight

The famous equestrian painting of Napoleon by David. *Reproduced by kind permission of the Mansell Collection* which followed, Turpin accidentally shot dead his companion. According to *Rookwood* it was after this affair that Turpin made the ride to York while escaping from his pursuers. The description of the ride has never been bettered since Ainsworth wrote it and it makes a dashing finale to his novel.

The harsh facts, though, are that after the attempted robbery of 'White Stockings', Turpin disappeared for a while and then reappeared in Yorkshire under the name of 'Palmer' and in the rôle of a country gentleman. The ruse did not work and Turpin was arrested and hanged at York on April 7th, 1739.

The fate of Black Bess, Turpin's one true friend, is not known; and it is this that suggests that Turpin's ride never took place, for surely a horse which could make such a journey to York would have been fêted for the rest of its life.

Copenhagen was a horse born to become famous, but only through its master — the Duke of Wellington. The Duke bought Copenhagen in 1812 and rode him throughout the Peninsular Campaign. The appearance of the dashing Duke riding the equally impressive Copenhagen lifted the morale of many of the British troops during bitter moments of action.

Copenhagen was a distinctive horse and it was partly for that reason that the Duke made the greatest use of him — in those days the appearance of the generals of the troops was essential to morale and the more colourful the military leaders looked on their horses, the better for the campaign.

Copenhagen also showed other qualities apart from his beauty. He carried the Duke of Wellington throughout the Battle of Waterloo. By the sixteenth hour of the Battle, Copenhagen, it was said, was looking fitter than his master, who was beginning to feel the strain of the battle. In fact, the Duke praises Copenhagen in his diaries on that occasion.

In the years of peace which followed, the gallant Copenhagen was retired to Stratfield Saye with Wellington. There his task was simpler and far more fitting to an animal of his grace — namely to give rides to favoured lady friends of the Duke. But the friendship the Duke had for Copenhagen was not matched by that of the ladies, for they found the horse far too frisky for their ride to be enjoyable: Copenhagen had retained the fire which he had displayed in battle.

This great horse was buried at Stratfield Saye with full military honours and lies under a headstone inscribed:

'God's humble instrument, though meaner clay,
Should share the glory of that glorious day.'

128

HORSES IN THE
CIRCUS

The orchestra played music from Borodin's 'Prince Igor', barbaric and suggestive of snow-swept Russian steppes. Into the circus ring drove a sleigh, drawn by three grey Arabian horses. The driver was a woman of exceptional beauty, jewelled and dressed in white furs. Escorting her were two men in the uniform of Cossack officers; they rode chestnut stallions, powerful and full of fire. In the glare of the

Douglas Eastwood

Pauline Schumann with the famous Schumann Greys. *Reproduced by kind permission of the Circus Schumann*

129

Albert Schumann with his highly trained Arab, Attila. *Reproduced by kind permission of the Circus Schumann*

spotlights the horses circled the ring, performing flawlessly the classic movements of the *haute-école*.

Very few of those watching in the audience appreciated the finer points of the horsemanship: the levades, the piaffe, the courbettes and the stately marche espagnole. What they did appreciate was the artistry of the whole presentation. Everything — costumes, horses, music arrangement and quality of training — added up to a circus masterpiece.

The riders in this act were Albert and Max Schumann, with Albert's Spanish wife Pauline driving the greys. Generations of Schumanns have trained horses for the circus; where Schumanns are concerned, nothing short of perfection will suffice. Schumann training is never hurried. Most circus trainers nowadays use poorly trained horses in the ring because, they say, they haven't any option. A circus horse starts to earn his keep only when he has learned to perform in public and thorough training is a long and costly business.

A century and a half ago, things were different. Those were the days of the Golden Age of the circus horse. Horsemen like François Baucher and Laurent Franconi thrilled circus audiences with the sheer beauty and mastery of their performances. Life then lacked the mad sense of urgency that prevails nowadays: horses were trained carefully and lovingly, and time was no object. As a result, perfection in equine acts was the order of the day — a perfection only rarely glimpsed in the modern circus.

Britain can be proud of the fact that the circus was founded by an Englishman. In the spring of 1768, Philip Astley opened the world's first circus in Lambeth, between the bridges of Westminster and Blackfriars. Far removed from the enormous circus spectacles we know today, Astley's circus consisted mainly of riding feats perfomed by the proprietor himself. Musical accompaniment was provided by Mrs Astley beating a drum. The publicity side of the business was handled by Philip Astley too: he rode through the London streets on his white charger, handing out advertising leaflets.

130

Although England saw the first circus horses, it was on the Continent during the last century that the circus horse achieved full glory. One noted circus owner, who was also a magnificent horseman, combined the skill of a great rider with the soul of a poet. One of his acts consisted of four coal black English stallions trained to work together in a high-school routine. They were ridden by four slim girls, all brunettes selected for their good looks. Circus critics acclaimed the act as a master-piece.

Today there are still superb horse acts to be seen in the circus from time to time. Fredy Knie, of the Swiss Circus Knie, has several wonderful groups of liberty horses. His team of white Lipizzaner stallions, plumed in violet feathers and bearing gold crowns on their harness, is a sight not easily forgotten. Fredy also has groups

Astley's circus, the first in the world, where equestrian acts were the main attraction

of grey Portuguese horses, heavy black French horses, spotted Knapstruppers, and a newly acquired team of chestnut Polish-bred Arabs, twelve in number. This last troupe appeared recently at the Tower Circus, Blackpool, presented by the trainer Sacha Houcke. Full of energy and high spirits, yet obedient to Sacha's whips, this was the finest liberty act I had seen in years.

A spectacular number featuring forty-eight horses was presented by Franz Althoff in Germany recently. Consisting of Lipizzaner, Arabian, black Fresian, Pinzgauer and Oldenburger horses, the act worked in an outsize arena instead of the normal ring, which is 42 feet in diameter. The handling of such a huge group of animals calls for horsemastery of the first order.

One of Fredy Knie's spotted Knapstruppers. *Reproduced by kind permission of the Blackpool Tower Circus*

The Circus Krone uses the famous Lipizzaner breed of horses that are used by the Spanish Riding School. *Reproduced by kind permission of the Circus Krone*

Another German show boasting horse acts of high quality is that of Krone. Circus Krone features a group of 24 Lipizzaner horses in a liberty routine. A great pet with the Krone show is Pegasus, a horse with a coat which is the colour of a new penny. Programmed as 'the golden horse', Pegasus performs a see-saw act in partnership with his elephant friend Lony.

As I write, the French Cirque Amar is touring Austria. Topping the bill with this show is Jose Moeser, a high-school rider. Moeser uses four horses in his number, each being trained to specialise in different airs. Certain of the animals perform the ground airs of the *haute-école*, such as piaffe and passage. Others work in the more spectacular leaping or 'off the ground' airs, like the capriole. Two of Jose's mounts are French bred horses, Realtor and Vic du Verdier; the others are Pluto Servola, a magnificent Lipizzaner, and Cordoba, an Andalusian stallion.

One of the finest circus horsemen in the world, Moeser has never appeared in Britain except for a short season in the Isle of Man, a few years ago. 'The British shows never offer me enough money,' he told me. Jose Moeser is a gentleman farmer besides being a circus rider. He trains his horses leisurely and exhibits them in public only when they have attained the high standard he requires. All Moeser's mounts are muscular, powerful animals. Jose himself is over six feet in height; apart from being a wonderful rider he is a fine showman. He invariably wears Mexican costume when showing his horses in the ring.

Another great showman and a good friend is Derrick Rosaire. Derrick and his two horses are now working in America. They perform an 'educated' act. At one time this kind of act was popular with the small family circuses that toured the

133

Sixteen of Bertram Mills' chestnut horses in a spectacular act. *Reproduced by kind permission of Bertram Mills' Circus*

country-side. It consisted of such simple tricks as a horse shaking its head to indicate 'yes' or 'no', counting by pawing with a hoof, and so on. By streamlining this type of routine and bringing it up to date to fit into the fast tempo of a modern circus programme, Derrick has achieved enormous success. In recent years he has starred with most of the top shows in Europe. Tony, the horse Derrick first trained to this routine, was an incredibly knowing animal. Occasionally the trainer would miss a cue during the performance; usually this is enough to throw any animal act out of gear. Tony, however, scathingly ignored his trainer's mistakes and continued the act in its correct sequence. 'Sometimes,' Derrick told me, 'I begin to wonder whether I'm showing the horse or the horse is showing me.'

Horsemanship is one of the highlights of the famous Moscow State Circus. At Ivanovo in the Soviet Union is a training school for circus riders. Under the direction of veteran horsemen such as Alexander Serge, the head of the school, young riders learn the intricacies of bareback and cossack routines. The difficult horse-to-horse back somersault (in which the rider, standing on the rump of one horse, somersaults to land on his feet on a second horse following behind) has been achieved recently by the young Soviet equestrians Victor Loguinov, Vladimir Teplov and others. The same trick has been featured by the Enrico Caroli troupe of Italian riders, and more recently by a young German circus star, Addy Enders.

Typical of the fast cossack routines favoured by the Moscow Circus are those presented by Les Kalganov, a team of horsemen working at great speed and riding swift, exotically caparisoned horses; and the Kochenovy troupe, who recently appeared in London in an act consisting of cossack games on horseback. I personally did not care much for this last number. I prefer the more orthodox type of circus riding act.

In America, alas, the circus horse is not flourishing. The big American circuses tend to regard the hose as a back number insofar as show business is concerned.

134

In a recent season one of the biggest American shows featured only two horses in the programme. These were indifferently bred and their standard of training was very poor. This decline in horse numbers has occurred since the war. Pre-war, some American shows used spectacular equine acts, such as the big troupe of Palomino horses trained by Jorgen Christiansen, or the intrepid Dorothy Herbert, who rode a black stallion over flaming barriers, riding sidesaddle and accompanied by a herd of riderless horses.

Pre-war, too, such riders as Roberto Vasconcellos starred with the high-school horses with the American circuses. Nowadays, in the raucous atmosphere of the American arenas, the beauty and the quiet dignity of the skilled horseman has yielded place to the bevies of chorus girls and the blonde beauties fired twice nightly from a huge cannon.

In Britain, the finest circus studs are to be found at Bertram Mills' Circus, Billy Smart's Circus and, each summer season, at the Blackpool Tower Circus.

Bertram Mills' famous liberty horses. *Reproduced by kind permission of Bertram Mills' Circus*

'. . . horses *are* the circus.'

Bertram Mills' favour Arabs for their liberty acts. At present they have teams of eight greys and eight chestnuts. Smarts seem to prefer big, heavy black Dutch horses. A bit cumbersome in action, these blacks are nevertheless beautiful. In the ring they wear yellow harness, accentuating the ebony gleam of their coats.

Nowadays, circus owners are perpetually in search of new gimmicks to 'sell' their liberty horse acts. There is a belief that the circus-going public gets bored with seeing the same type of routine in horse acts. Consequently we find horses wearing harness treated with luminous paint, others with dummy riders strapped to their backs. The other day I watched a team of superb Lipizzaner stallions working in a liberty routine; the animals were covered from head to tail in elaborate drapings. Instead of highly bred stallions the trainer might just as well have used mules, for all the audience saw of them. To make things worse, much of the routine was performed in darkness. Fascinating as it may be to watch twelve sets of luminous harness moving around the ring, it is no compensation for seeing the horses themselves. The keynote of a good circus equine act is simplicity. If a trainer uses top quality animals, adequately trained, gimmicks are superfluous.

Not all horses in the circus are employed in liberty riding acts. Occasionally one comes across a 'balloon horse'. These animals are trained to stand stock still as they are hoisted into the dome of the circus on a small platform carrying a rider.

At the climax of the routine horse and rider are surrounded by cascades of fireworks. This type of number requires an animal with a docile temperament and no nerves.

Horses and wild beasts often work in partnership in the sawdust ring. Soviet trainer Irena Bugrimova taught a huge lion to career around the ring on horseback. Fredy Hager recently presented a hyena riding a white stallion with Cirque Francki in France. Bears and mountain lions, too, have appeared as equestrians in the circus. Not long ago, Harry Belli exhibited a horse-riding tiger with the Dutch Strassburger Circus. Two dogs appeared in this act also — all four animals working happily together.

Although horses employed in this kind of act are always armoured with a type of chain mail (in case the wild beast rider slips and claws at the horse to regain balance) some circus owners refuse to feature such acts because of the element of danger to the horse.

Horses were the beginning of the circus. No matter what role they play in the ring, horses are the very lifeblood of the circus. The breathtaking beauty we find in horses is emphasised in the sawdust ring by gay trappings, music and spotlights. Horses may have disappeared from our daily life to a large extent. I do not believe they will ever disappear from the circus, simply because horses *are* the circus.

'Careful — that stung!' *Reproduced by kind permission of 'Punch'*

HORSES IN

G. S. Whittet

The horse was the subject of art almost before man himself. In the earliest examples of the mural artist — at Altamira, Font-de-Gaume, Les Combarelles, La Mouthe, Niaux, all in the area of south-west France and northern Spain and belonging to the Palaeolithic age — the form of the horse is drawn with varying degrees of naturalism, but all of the drawings are obviously the result of keen observation.

Perhaps best-known of the sites of this so-called cave art is Lascaux in the Dordognes, discovered accidentally by some schoolboys in 1940. Since then, much has been written about the wonderful paintings and engravings that were brought to modern knowledge after some twenty to thirty thousand years in darkness. The difficulty of photography and lighting them has left many of their beauties still unreproduced, although an English artist, Douglas Mazonowitz, has done much to reveal the colour and composition of these large sections of the cave walls and roof by excellent full-scale copies in silk-screen prints. Among them are the frieze of little horses and the so-called 'Chinese' horse, though the details closely resemble those of Przewalski's horse, which is today living in a wild state in Mongolia.

The purpose of this cave art by Upper Palaeolithic man was a magic one, of propitiating the powers of the unknown so that they would assist him in the hunt

The 'Frieze of Little Horses' in the Lascaux Caves, from a copy made by Douglas Mazonowitz. *Reproduced by kind permission of St George's Gallery*

Above: 17th century Indian miniature

19th century Persian miniature. *Reproduced by kind permission of the Trustees of the British Museum*

'The Infant Balthasar Carlos' by Velasquez. *Reproduced by kind permission of the Prado, Madrid*

'John Viscount St Asaph' by Tillemans. *Reproduced by kind permission of the Rev. John Bickersteth*

'Mares and Foals' by Stubbs. *Reproduced by kind permission of the Trustees of the Tate Gallery*

'Guidoriccio da Fogliano' by Simone Martini. *Reproduced by kind permission of the Ente Provinciale Turismo, Siena*

'Horses' by Hokusai. *Reproduced by kind permission of the Bibliothèque Nationale, Paris*

for animals, of which the horse was one — that it was pursued for its edible qualities is obvious from the drawings, which show spears impaling it, and from the models in clay in which javelin thrusts are apparent. Not all the horses are shown in large scale — some of the finest drawing was done as engravings on ivory and a reindeer's horn.

After prehistoric art, which extended through several millenia in scattered centres, it is only when we come to the Nile valley that we find an unbroken record of art traceable back to the beginning of history, almost 4,000 years before the Christian era. Yet although there are animated scenes of many different animals, in the decorative reliefs on the back of rouge palettes, the horse is not among them. Donkeys appear as beasts of burden in tomb paintings, but the horse is not depicted until about the time of the fourteenth dynasty, when the struggle against the Hyksos first brought the horse into Egyptian life. Here it was used for warfare and hunting, and was always harnessed to a chariot. On a relief carving from a Memphite tomb that is in the Museo Civico, Bologna, we first encounter the rider — a boy bareback on a horse. In a massive composition on the outer wall of the Hypostyle Hall at Karnak, the King Sety I figures towering in his chariot drawn by two rampant horses, while before him tumble infantry and chariotborne soldiers of the Syrian Army, whose defeat is commemorated.

On the lid of a chest from his tomb, which was discovered in 1922, Tut-Ankh-Amon, famous king, is shown as a hunter of prowess, in a chariot drawn by two horses in profiled plunge. Arrows from his drawn bow are stuck in the herd of panic-stricken deer before him. If the horses' pose seems stiff and theatrical, it should be remembered that for the greater part of their history in world art horses have been conventionalised to a degree never resorted to with humans.

As the horse first appeared in Egypt from Asia Minor, it is not surprising that we find it figuring further east in the art of Mesopotamia. The Assyrians excelled in painting and carving horses. From 4000 B.C. there survives a shell cylinder on which are engraved horses and chariots engaged in battle. On the bronze reliefs from the Gates of Shalmaneser II in the British Museum, we see horses crossing a river on a pontoon bridge. As in Egypt, the horses are shown drawing chariots, and it was not until the ninth century B.C. that mounted men were painted. One of the finest alabaster reliefs from the seventh century B.C. is of King Ashurbanipal hunting lions, his horse in the pose known as the extended plunge, while the royal rider draws his bow.

In the Islamic art of Persia the glories of the sculpture in the reliefs at Persepolis of about the fifth century B.C., showing horses being lead and drawing chariots, were never repeated. It was in the miniature arts that the Persians excelled — in metal ware, the cameo and the illuminated manuscript, especially the latter. During the fifteenth and sixteenth centuries painting reached its highest peak. Bihzad (1450-1525) was the creator of a brilliant school, and Shah Tahmasp,

Egyptian painting of horse and chariot. *Reproduced by kind permission of the Trustees of the British Museum*

Shah Ismail, Sultan Mohammed and Mirak are among his outstanding successors. Horses abound in the miniature paintings that illustrate such manuscripts as the Poems of Nizami, a masterpiece of the sixteenth century in the British Museum. Persian artists were the first to depict polo.

Echoes of Persian prototypes are to be seen in the earliest rendering of the horse in India, where it takes its place as a Buddhist symbol in the monolithic columns erected in about 240 B.C. during the reign of the Emperor Asoka at Sarnath. Some of the finest Buddhist works in relief were found at Amaravati, of which a panel from the Stupa is in the British Museum depicting fighting horses, although it must be admitted that elephants, the royal animals, are modelled more faithfully than horses. But, as in Persia, the most notable portrayals of the horse are in illuminated manuscripts, including many for the Moghul Emperors who brought illustrators from Persia and established an interchange of artists between the two territories. Jahangir (1605-1627) and his successor Shah Jahan and his sons are subjects of many miniatures, in which they are painted mounted on elegantly profiled horses, their saddlecloths displaying intricate detail.

In the long and continuous Chinese culture, horses recur with regularity. Two of the earliest, expertly worked in three-dimensional bronze, date from the late Chou Dynasty (about the sixth to the third century B.C.) and show a bulky type

144

Assyrian bas relief of King Ashurbanipal shooting lions from the saddle. *Reproduced by kind permission of the Trustees of the British Museum*

of animal, solid and strongly built. During the Han Dynasty (202 B.C. to A.D. 221) horses are frequently included in the reliefs carved on funeral shrines, often in the animated 'extended plunge'. In sculpture one of the best-known horses is carved in stone before the tomb of Ho Ch'u-ping, Shensi, who died about 117 B.C. It is in the act of trampling upon a barbarian, surely one of the cruellest records of 'man's best friend'. Pottery and tiles of the Han are decorated with horses in violent movement, and the jade carvings, including one exquisite fragment with high-arched neck in the Victoria and Albert Museum, are spirited evocations in stylised imagery. Power and energetic tension are presented in the painted pottery horses of the Six Dynasties (265-587), and the T'ang pottery horses (618-906) are world-famous for their compact form. From this period comes the handscroll ink drawing of 'Shining Light of the Night', a favourite horse of T'ang Ming Huang, by Han Kan, in which a startled beast rears back against a post.

A relief from Persepolis showing subjects bringing gifts. *Reproduced by kind permission of Rostamy, Teheran Museum*

145

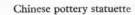
Chinese pottery statuette

But it is in the Yuan Dynasty that China had her Munnings. Chao Meng-Fu (1254-1322) was an artist who became Cabinet Minister at the court of the Mongo conqueror Kubla Khan, and in his handscrolls he painted horses in ink and slight colours in composition of interlinking incident and background.

Returning West to the Mediterranean, and to the root source of European culture, we find in Greece some of the greatest expressions of humanist art. In the classical period, the horse is rendered on a scale and with a dignity that almost brings it on to a par with mankind. Centaurs abound, and in their composition of half-horse and half-man there seems no absurdity. In the sanctuaries and tombs from about 900 to 580 B.C. small terra cotta horses are plentiful, mostly modelled by hand, among them a group from Beotia of the seventh century B.C., where four little horses, feet four square on the ground yet with heads and necks poised, stand before a light chariot bearing two warriors.

Pottery takes the place of the painted wall and panel in Greek history, since only it has survived in quantity. From the eighth century B.C. come vases decorated with wiry line drawings of warriors in horse-drawn chariots. The style of the period shows an oriental influence, and by the middle of the seventh century B.C. we find horses in crude but vivid force. Vigorous battle scenes in black figure ware exists in the latter half of the sixth century.

Probably the greatest pieces of Greek sculpture are those from the frieze of the Parthenon. The Horse of Selene, the Moon, is a boldly chiselled figure that aims at naturalism. The frieze, which ran along the four sides of the building for more than 500 feet, takes as its subject the Panathenaia, the great Athenian festival. The riders mount and proceed in cavalcade to meet the procession of maidens; the climax is in the handing over of the *peplos,* the new robe, for Athena in the pres-

146

ence of the gods. Dating from 442-438 B.C. the design of the sculpture is attributed to Pheidias. His reliefs of riders give us an impression of equestrian movement that is unequalled in the world, and one hundred horses can be counted in the frieze of the Parthenon.

From Greek to Roman art was a natural transition. While many Roman copies of Greek originals existed, there was a movement of Greek artists to Italy during the first century A.D. when Greece was conquered. First of the great equestrian statues was that of the Emperor Marcus Aurelius executed about 200 B.C. and moved to its site on the Capitoline Hill at the request of Michelangelo in 1538, when he designed the Piazza. Some of the early Roman work is extant in the carvings on Trajan's column (dedicated A.D. 114), where horses bearing soldiers are depicted in low relief.

In medieval times the horse takes its place in manuscript and tapestry with all the importance that is its due. In the most famous work of embroidery in the world — the Bayeux Tapestry, executed about the year 1080 and telling the story of the Norman Conquest — we see William the Conqueror mounted on his Castilian Arab stallion. In all, more than two hundred horses are worked in somewhat crude drawing, but without a monotonous repetition in the 231 feet of its length.

From early in the fourteenth century can be seen beautiful examples of the miniaturist's art in illuminated manuscripts such as 'Queen Mary's Psalter', where

Detail from the Parthenon frieze. *Reproduced by kind permission of the Trustees of the British Museum*

William of Hainault setting out on his expedition against Friesland, Harley MSS. *Reproduced by kind permission of the Trustees of the British Museum*

a hawking party, including two women riding astride, provides a playful footnote to the religious picture painted on the page above. About this time the craft of the ivory carver flourished too and there are in existence many similar scenes of hunting parties encompassed in the small circular shape of a mirror back. Horses ridden by members of the court are familiar subjects in the celebrated 'Books of the Hours' painted by Paul and Jean de Limbourg for the Burgundian Duc de Berry.

St Francis, the monk whose love for animals set the spiritual climate for the Renaissance, is appropriately the subject of a fresco painted by Giotto in the Upper Church of Assisi as riding a horse. Simone Martini (*c.* 1283-1344) will be honoured by horse lovers for his alert mount in the life-size fresco of Guido-riccio da Fogliano in the Palazzo Pubblico, Siena, colourfully caparisoned and stepping briskly. But it is in the religious painting of the fifteenth and sixteenth centuries that Italian painting is so rich in representations of the horse, in scenes of the Adoration and renderings of St George, St Martin and St Hubert.

Pisanello (1385-1455) was a prolific animal painter, whose 'Vision of St Eustace' and 'Virgin and Child with St George and St Anthony' prove his prowess. Paolo Uccello (1396-1475) was one of the first to investigate the problem of perspective, and his 'Rout of San Romano' in the National Gallery, with its 'papery' cavalry is famous. Botticelli (1440-1510) and Giorgione (c. 1478-1510), each of whom painted 'The Adoration of the Kings', treated their horse figures with respect.

Leonardo da Vinci (1452-1519), himself a horseman, was the genius of the Renaissance whose mind outran his energy and he left few completed masterpieces, although there is in an English collection a bronze statuette of a horse that is possibly by his hand. His drawings of horses reveal his complete knowledge of its body's articulation and muscles. Titian (1477-1576) was the Grand Master of Venice and his horses took on the dignity and grandeur of all his work, notably in the famous equestrian portait of Charles V, even if the anatomy has its short-comings.

Sculptors in Italy have left a heritage that is unrivalled elsewhere in the Christian era. Lorenzo Ghiberti's (1378-1455) bronze doors for the Baptistry, Florence, are beyond praise for their delicacy and wealth of detail, which includes the heads of horses life-like in tiny scale. In Padua is the bronze 'Gattamelata' of Donatello (1386-1466) which in its classic pose recalls the Roman statue of Marcus Aurelius. The second masterpiece of the Renaissance is by Verrocchio (1435-1488), whose 'Colleoni' in Venice is unforgettable in its spirited movement and dramatic pose of the rider.

'Study of horses', a drawing by Leonardo da Vinci. *Reproduced by gracious permission of Her Majesty the Queen*

In the paintings of the artists of the Low Countries, the horse plays only a small part in the composition, where its place is incidental. The Van Eycks, for example, treat the subject best in the lower panels of the left wing of their famous altar piece of the Holy Lamb in St Bavon, Ghent (completed in 1432). The riders in the foreground, representing the 'Just Judges' and the 'Knights of Christ', are mounted on trim steeds each with a rear and fore leg raised. The pictures of Pieter Brueghel the Elder are thickly populated with people, and when horses do appear they have a sturdy Flemish look, as in 'The Conversion of St Paul' and 'The Massacre of the Innocents' and his drawing of a team of work horses.

Peter Paul Rubens (1577-1640), inventive and prolific, painted as many equestrian portraits as any artist who ever lived — his travels on diplomatic business throughout Europe brought him many commissions, though one of his best renderings of horses is in the detail of his home, 'The Château de Stern'. Jan Fyt was also a great painter of horses and one of the first to make them the sole subject of a painting.

Sir Anthony van Dyck (1599-1641), like Rubens, used the horses as a studio 'property' on which to present his sitters: certainly in his two portraits of Charles I on horseback the monarch comes off best by comparison. Rembrandt (1606-1669) seldom attempted to paint horses. But the painting of his son mounted and dressed up as 'The Polish Rider' provoked the comment from Sickert when he saw it in London in 1910: 'one of the perfect masterpieces of the world'. Peter Tillemans (1684-1734), another Flemish painter, who settled in England, has succeeded in giving a likeness to his horses no less than to his riders, as the portrait of Viscount St Asaph clearly shows.

German art contains no great names of equestrian painters, although Albrecht Dürer (1471-1528), in his equestrian engravings and woodcuts, displays in thin nervous line his controlled grasp of form and keen observation of horses.

Among the Spanish masters El Greco, in his equestrian painting of 'St Martin and the Beggar', considerably elongates the shapes of the figures and the horse, but nevertheless achieves a beautiful effect. It is Velasquez (1599-1690) who stands paramount as the delineator of the horse, whether it be in the cheerful lively mount of the Infante Balthasar Carlos or in the splendid silky quarters of the victorious commander's horse in 'The Surrender of Breda'.

Left: Colleoni statue by Verrocchio

Opposite: A sketch for the painting of Charles I on horseback by Van Dyck. *Reproduced by gracious permission of Her Majesty the Queen*

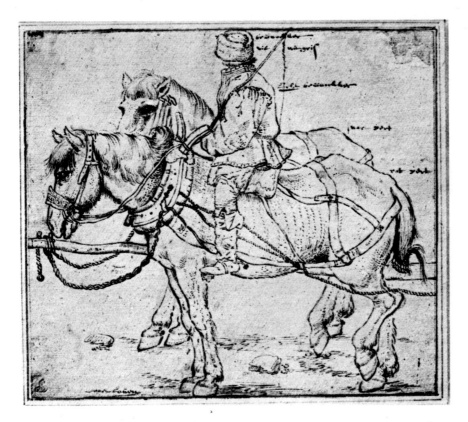

'A team of horses', by Pieter Brueghel the Elder. *Reproduced by kind permission of the Öster-reichische Nationalbibliothek*

By the French, equine form is better served. François Clouet (1505-1572) could record as faithfully as a camera every detail of armour and accoutrement in the portrait of François I of France and still leave some life in the horse. Another ruler of France — Napoleon — is immortalised by Jacques Louis David (1748-1823) in a painting that emphasises only too faithfully the First Consul's bad horsemanship, while dramatising his 'Excelsior' pose astride his famous grey Marengo.

Théodore Géricault (1791-1824) was a precursor of the Romantic Movement, although in fact he painted horses with a realism unknown until then. Delacroix (1799-1863), who emerged as leader of the Romantics, invested all his subjects, including horses, with a fire and fury of colour that whips up the emotional response to such scenes of mounted combat as 'The Giaour and the Pasha' and 'The Lion Hunt'. Rosa Bonheur (1822-1899) has a place in history as the painter of 'Horses Threshing Corn' with ten life-size horses, surely the biggest animal picture ever created. Jean Louis Meissonier (1815-1891), who knew much about horses, was the diligent illustrator of Napoleon's campaigns.

Coming to modern times, most of the Impressionists found horses too full of movement to reflect light, but Degas painted several race track and hunting

'A Courier' by Dürer. *Reproduced by kind permission of the Trustees of the British Museum*

'The Polish Trumpeter' by Géricault. *Reproduced by kind permission of the Burrell Collection,*
Glasgow Art Gallery

scenes with an eye for the physical articulation in horse and rider that he found
in dancers and laundresses. Henri de Toulouse-Lautrec, son of a French count
who was never long out of the saddle, was a draughtsman of intense elegance and
expressed the controlled dynamic energy of the racehorse with born genius.

In British art, the prolific number of horse paintings makes other subjects seem
almost neglected by comparison. The love of hunting and its allied sport, horse-
racing, has encouraged the decoration of country houses by horse paintings whose
size and treatment suggest an attitude to the horse not far short of idolatry. Francis
Barlow was one of the earliest English artists who painted a racehorse — he was
born in the 1620's — but it was in the following century that the sporting artist
really came into his own. John Wootton (1680-1756), who visited Italy and suc-

153

'The Horsemen' by Daumier. *Reproduced by kind permission of the Museum of Fine Arts, Boston*

cumbed to the influence of Italian landscape painting, acquired a rare pictorial background missing from some artists who became known chiefly as horse portraitists. One of the best of these was James Seymour (1702-1752), who painted horses with an eye to detail and a feeling for their finer points that endears him to horselovers, although art historians label him a 'primitive'.

George Stubbs (1724-1806), through the quality and popularity of his horse paintings, is hailed by posterity as 'the Master of the Horse'. Although he was, in fact, an equally good painter of other animals. His study of animal anatomy gave his later pictures a solidity of form that was lacking in his earlier paintings, with their romantic atmosphere of landscape.

Contemporary with him were talented artists like Sawrey Gilpin R. A. (1733-1807) and Francis Sartorius (1735-1804). The subjects of horses and their owners and families found a ready market in these times and a painter of country life such as George Morland (1763-1804) established a great demand for prints taken from his original paintings. Ben Marshall (1767-1835) was a portrait painter who began with humans and went on to include horses, whose anatomy he studied and observed with sometimes too rigorous an accuracy. He could, however, give great presence to a horse such as 'Phosphorus', as few others could.

154

'Le Jockey', a lithograph by Toulouse-Lautrec. *Reproduced by kind permission of the Print Department, Boston Public Library*

A painting by George Stubbs of the Prince of Wales out riding

James Ward R. A. (1769-1859) was one of England's leading Romantic painters, whose brother-in-law George Morland exercised some influence on him, although he admired Rubens more. His huge painting of the 'Triumph of Wellington', with the Duke in a coach drawn by four white horses, has disappeared — not without some difficulty, it must be supposed, since it reputedly measured 22 by 35 feet.

James Pollard (1772-1867) was one of the many painters who created the sporting prints that enjoy a wide popularity even to this day. John Ferneley (1782-1860), the famous Alken family and J. F. Herring (1795-1865) were painters much in demand during their lives, but soon after their deaths a decline set in their kind of art, although their paintings are still much prized by lovers of horse art. Sir Edwin Landseer (1802-1873), though renowned for his stags, could paint horses comparably well.

The swan song of the horse in art has probably been sung by Sir Alfred Munnings, P. P. R. A., because he marks, too, the passing of a way of life. Modern artists like Picasso in his 'Guernica' and the Italian sculptor Marini in his 'Horse and Rider' impose a distortion on their forms that tell us more of their creators than their models.

156

From Lascaux to the School of Paris, the horse has been ridden by artists a long, long way. The automobile and the aircraft, although they have ousted the horse from the social scene, have also brought increasing value to his pictures in the sale rooms of the world.

Munnings: 'Study of a Start'. *Reproduced by kind permission of Lady Munnings*

ACKNOWLEDGEMENTS

Acknowledgements are gratefully due to the following for permission to reproduce photographs. The numbers refer to pages: H. Armstrong Roberts: 108, 109, 110, 111. Arts Council: 67. Associated Press Agency: 32, 43, 44, 45. Australian News and Information Bureau: 15, 104. Austrian State Tourist Dept.: 56. Barnaby's Picture Library: 60, 82. M. Best: 20. J. Bridel: 51, 57. British Transport Museum: 98. British Travel and Holidays Assn.: 40, 61, 62. Camera Press Agency: 19, 29, 99. Central Press Agency: 50, 51, 53. J. Coote: 24. Eagle Photos: 94. 'The Field': 101. Gala Film Distributors: 87. D. M. Goodall: 91. Greyhound Racing Assn.: 50. G. Hammond: 14. E. O. Hoppé: 13, 136. Iceland Tourist Bureau: 18. Illustrated London News: 96. Independent Newspapers Ltd.: 52. Keystone Press Agency: 6, 8, 17, 42, 46, 48, 50, 53, 58, 66, 77, 83, 95, 96, 102, 106. Harold M. Lambert: 16. L. Mattock: 59. M-G-M Pictures: 74, 79, 86. Mirrorpic: 106. K. Money: 9, 81. H. Morton: 21, 22, 80, 120, 121. National Film Archive: 76, 84, 85. J. Nestle: 10, 11, 12, 39, 41. P. A. - Reuter: 94. J. Peterson: 23. Photographie Giraudon: 160. Pictorial Press Agency: 97. F. Pitt: 18. Pony/Light Horse: 25. Radio Times Hulton Picture Library: 92, 105, 122, 131, 156. Sport and General Press Agency: 30, 31, 34, 35, 36, 37, 38, 49, 51, 53, 54, 55. J. Topham: 93, 98. United-Artists: 84. Walt Disney Productions: 78. Whitbread and Co. Ltd.: 100.

Fore's Hunting Casualties: 'Dispatched to Head Quarters' by H. Alken. *Reproduced by kind permission of Fores Ltd*

Fore's Hunting Accomplishments: 'Charging an Ox Fence' by H. Alken. *Reproduced by kind permission of Fores Ltd*

'Setting off for the hunt' by Degas

'Phosphorus' by Ben Marshall. *Reproduced by kind permission of A. Ackermann & Son*